HOW TO REPEL POTENTIAL FRIENDS AND NOT INFLUENCE PEOPLE

THE EPIC WHALE OF A TALE FEATURING AMERICA'S SELF-PROCLAIMED MOST HUMBLE MALE

CLAYTRON MENENDEZ

How to Repel Potential Friends and Not Influence People
ISBN 978-1-7364217-0-3
Copyright © 2021 by Clay Clark

Thrive Publishing

Published by Thrive Publishing
1100 Suite #100 Riverwalk Terrace
Jenks, OK 74037

Printed in the United States of America. All rights reserved, because I called ahead. Printed in the United States of America. No part of this book may be used or reproduced in any manner whatsoever without written permission except in the case of brief quotations embodied in critical articles and reviews. For information, address Thrive Publishing, 1100 Riverwalk Terrace #1100, Jenks, OK, 74037.

Thrive Publishing books may be purchased for educational, business or sales promotional use. For more information, please email the Special Markets Department at info@ThriveTimeShow.com. For a good time visit ThriveTimeShow.com

CONTENTS

The Preamble (Drum Roll Please) 15

Chapter 1 19
If You Don't Want to Get Honey and You Want to Get Stung, Kick Over the Beehive

Chapter 2 25
Surround Yourself with Nefarious Idiots, Dramatic Dudes, Flaky Friends and Invest Your Time Trying to Change Them

Chapter 3 31
He Who Can Repel Everyone is Empowered to Sprint Naked Through the Toll Road of Life

Chapter 4 35
Provide Feedback and Criticism to People Who Aren't Asking for Your Advice

Chapter 5 39
Do This and You'll Make People Hate You

Chapter 6 43
A Great Way to a Bad First Impression

Chapter 7 45
ABL - Always Be Late (and Always Have an Excuse That You Believe for Being Late)

Chapter 8 51
If You Do This Move You Will Certainly Be On a Collision Course with Failure

Chapter 9 55
A Super-Move to Become a Dull Conversationalist

Chapter 10 59
How to Guarantee That People Instantly Don't Like You

Chapter 11 63
Email People Constantly 63

Chapter 12 65
You Can Win an Argument If You Yell Loud Enough

Chapter 13 67
The Best Way to Make an Enemy and How to Make Enemy Creation Unavoidable at all Times

Chapter 14 71
Get as Many Regrettable Tattoos as Possible While Angry, Depressed, Drunk or High

Chapter 15 75
A Spoonful of Drano Makes the Medicine Go Down

Chapter 16 79
Pet a Cat Backwards and Name it "Sh@# Head"

Chapter 17 83
No Matter What Just Happened, One Up Everybody in Their Moment of Triumph

Chapter 18 85
The Gasoline You Can Pour on the Fires of Complaints

Chapter 19 91
Make Problems Seem Unfixable and Dwell on Them without Trying to Solve Them

Chapter 20 95
The Magical Formula That Will Cause Even Sweet Elderly Christian Women to Give You "The Finger."

Chapter 21 99
What Nobody Wants

Chapter 22 103
An Appeal That Nobody Likes

Chapter 23 107
The Movies Don't Do It, Bishop T.D. Jakes Doesn't Do It. So Why Don't You Try It?

Chapter 24 111
When Something Is Not Working, Stay Loyal To It

Chapter 25 115
Be a Troll: How to Not Change People While Giving Great Offense and Stirring Up Resentment

Chapter 26 119
If You Must Find Fault, Start Off by Offending the Other Party.

Chapter 27 123
Focus On What They Did Wrong and Never Mention What You Have Ever Done Wrong

Chapter 28 127
Create a Yelp! Account and Invest Hours and Hours Into Becoming a Self-Proclaimed Restaurant Snob

Chapter 29 131
No One Likes to Take Orders, So Give Orders to People You Just Met, People You Have No Rapport with and People Who You Are Not in Charge of

Chapter 30 135
Don't Ever Let the Other Person Save Face

Chapter 31 139
How to Spur People Onto Failure

Chapter 32 143
The Big Secret of Repelling People

Chapter 33 147
Never Save Money and Always Live Above Your Means

Chapter 34 153
Practice Poor Hygiene When the Boss is Not Looking

Chapter 35 157
Conclusion: Choosing to Remain Poor Requires a Commitment to Jackassery

DISCLAIMER:

As Clay Clark's so-called "evil twin brother" I take a lot of crap from people in the family at the state unemployment offices for being constantly grumpy, negative, mopey, unemployed or "underemployed" for more than a decade now. However, it's now time for me to share my side of the story and why I've committed over a decade of life to researching *How to Repel Potential Friends and Not Influence People*. You see, I believe that my brother (Clay Clark), Napoleon Hill, Dale Carnegie, Daniel Goleman, Zig Zigler and others have written enough books about how to win friends and influence people. But, no one ever really invested the time to specifically lay out the steps you must take to *never* get ahead, to *never* gain traction with your career, and *repel* all potential friends and to influence anyone, ever.

You see when you are the "evil" twin-brother of somebody who is as successful as my brother (Clay Clark) you can't really become a writer of another self-help book because it will "never be as good as Clay's book." And so I'm well aware that we can all choose to become either choose to get bitter or better and I have chosen to become bitter. Consider Clay to be the Obi Wan Kenobi of self-help and I'm the Darth Vader of self-help. In fact as Clay has consistently taken the high road in route to winning business awards and to starting multi-million dollar companies (DJConnection.com, EITRLounge.com, EpicPhotos.com, MakeYourLifeEpic.com) as a result of knowing how to win friends and influence people, I have chosen to take the road most taken. My friend, I have chosen to take the low road. You see Gallup now reports that "70% of people hate their jobs" and Inc.

Magazine now reports that "96% of businesses fail within 10 years" and I have taken the time to study the most unsuccessful people on the planet, and to determine the common denominators that most unsuccessful people share. After investing years studying the worst of the worst, the biggest losers on the planet, I then decide to become a modern martyr for my work and test my theories on 34 super moves you must use to repel potential friends and not influence people. At times it was tough, but this literary gift that I present to you was worth every intentionally bad decision that I have chosen to make over this past decade.

Where as Clay has chosen to interview the world's most successful people on his Thrivetime Show podcast, and to distill their success strategies, proven systems and mechanical moves for mastery and achievement, I have chosen to study the worst people I could possibly find. For your benefit as the reader, for the sake of my research and in my humble attempt to provide you with proven strategies for *How to Repel Potential Friends and Not Influence People,* I have chosen to live a very different life and one that some would say is not worth writing about. However, I would disagree. I have tried to pattern my life after big-time frequent self-destructing personalities such as Charlie Sheen, Antonio Brown, and Miley Cyrus. My life for this past decade has really been about sacrifice and choosing to not be nice so that I could ruin my life like hair when it has lice.

WHY DID I WRITE THIS BOOK?

As I think about the profundity of this book, I am overwhelmed by its immensity and I feel called to down a shot of scotch on the rocks just to take the nervousness out of this moment, as I realize that you and I are now reading this incredible literary wonder that I have birthed. My friend, I feel as though this book is almost as important as the man who wrote it. You see, in this world where teen moms are celebrated and marketed and are given their own reality TV shows on MTV, and where Kim Kardashian was able to launch herself into super stardom as a result of "accidentally" intentionally leaking her own sex tape, I thought this book would fit right in and would provide you with the absolute truth about *How to Repel Potential Friends and Not Influence People*.

A BOOK FILLED WITH "TRUTHI-NESS" FOR A WORLD THAT LOVES "FAKE NEWS"

In this world where nobody fact checks the insane headlines being produced by attention-craving "Social Media-ites", and where fake reality shows and "fake news" are devoured all day every day by smartphone users committed to being dumb, I knew that this planet would love a book filled with the kind of "truthi-ness" and situational honesty that I bring to table. It is true that you could spend your nights and weekends attempting to verify the various facts that fill the pages of this book that some would label as fiction. However, I would argue that it's actually more fun to kill time by going to the casino and watch poor old people hooked up to oxygen tanks smoke as they play "The Wheel of Fortune", and "Britney Spears" themed slot machines while they rant out how "the rich just get richer" and how "the buffett" and "the show" is really why they have traveled 3 hours to The WinStar World Casino in Thackerville, Oklahoma which now calls itself "The largest casino in the world." Feel free to use this bonus tip whenever you are needing to kill time as poor people often do.

NOTABLE QUOTABLE

"Determine never to be idle. No person will have occasion to complain of the want of time who never loses any. It is wonderful how much can be done if we are always doing."

– THOMAS JEFFERSON

(An American statesman who during his 83 years on the planet became a successful diplomat, lawyer, architect, philosopher, and the Founding Father who served as the third president of the United States from 1801 to 1809. In his downtime he also previously served as the second vice president of the United States from 1797 to 1801. And because he did not waste his time going to Casinos and spending his day consuming social media was also able to be the principal author of the Declaration of Independence. Jefferson was my kind of guy and a proponent of democracy, republicanism, and individual rights, motivating American colonists to break from the Kingdom of Great Britain and form a new nation.)

In order to get this book published I had to make certain compromises, one of which was to my brother (Clay Clark) to insert his favorite notable quotables, and facts throughout the text that will teach you how to win friends and influence people, but that should allow us to get distracted because my main focus of this book here is to teach you *How to Repel Potential Friends and Not Influence People.* I hear people always discussing and debate about whether success is a matter of luck or not, and yet don't often hear about whether poverty in America is a choice or not. I hope this book gives you the facts that you need to know to go out there and act like a jackass so that you too, can become broke like me. Consider these facts from the Thrivetime Show podcast guest, accountant and best-selling author, Tom Corley in his book, *The Habits of the Rich*:

- 1. 70% of wealthy eat less than 300 junk food calories per day. 97% of poor people eat more than 300 junk food calories per day.

- 2. 23% of wealthy gamble. 52% of poor people gamble.

- 3. 80% of wealthy are focused on accomplishing some single goal. Only 12% of the poor do this.

- 4. 76% of wealthy exercise aerobically 4 days a week. 23% of poor do this.

- 5. 63% of wealthy listen to audiobooks during commute to work vs. 5% for poor people.

- 6. 81% of wealthy maintain a to-do list vs. 19% for poor.

- 7. 67% of wealthy write down their goals vs. 17% for poor

- 8. 88% of wealthy read 30 minutes or more each day for education or career reasons vs 2% for poor.

- 9. 6% of wealthy say what's on their mind vs. 69% for poor.

- 10. 79% of wealthy network 5 hours or more each month vs. 16% for poor.

- 11. 67% of wealthy watch 1 hour or less of TV every day vs. 23% for poor

- 13. 6% of wealthy watch reality TV vs. 78% for poor.

- 14. 74% of wealthy teach good daily success habits to their children vs. 1% for poor.

15. 84% of wealthy believe good habits create opportunity luck vs. 4% for poor.

16. 76% of wealthy believe bad habits create detrimental luck vs. 9% for poor.

17. 86% of wealthy believe in life-long educational self-improvement vs. 5% for poor.

18. 86% of wealthy love to read vs. 26% for poor.

Really, the choice is yours. If you want to be unsuccessful, I know the moves. If you want to learn *How to Repel Potential Friends and Not Influence People*, I know the proven path. Do you want to do what my brother does, and become just another successful person who enjoys both time and financial freedom as a result of diligently implementing a proven path and become a person who is obsessed with self-discipline? No. You want to do what the masses are doing. You want to join the powerful pity party that I am organizing. Although at times you may struggle to believe the various stories I've included in this book, you must remember that I've invested nearly a decade of my life into writing this book and verifying with myself the various facts found within it based upon the various feelings I have, the situational honesty that I believe in, and the parables that I use to teach.

You may ask yourself, "How was I able to find the time needed to cover a subject so vast and deep?"

Well, when you don't have a vision, hope, or a job, you have a ton of time on your hands. And really, with my educational background, I'm "over-qualified" for most of the job offers that I receive, so I've been really just holding out for a management position for nearly a decade now.

Furthermore... if I were to go out and actually get a "rich job", I would lose government assistance, and you don't want to do that if you are focused on paving the path to the bottom.

IF CLAY CLARK AND I ARE TWIN BROTHERS, WHY AM I NAMED CLAYTRON MENENDEZ?

For the record, my birth name was once Tiberius Clark, but I chose to change my name to the stage name of Claytron Menendez, because the name "Trixie Menendez" was already taken, and because I wanted to be more politically correct to demonstrate my love for "those people" (if you know what I mean).

AMERICA'S MOST HUMBLE MAN
Claytron Menendez

A BRAVE NOTE FROM THE AUTHOR

It has taken me nearly 9 years to write the incredible words that you now hold in your hand, and that you are reading with your eyeballs. This most magnificent book is one that took me nearly 9 years to write because I chose to relentlessly do things that poor and unsuccessful people do to give you that real and raw first hand experience that readers trust and love. It turns out it's really hard to write a book when you are interacting with your smartphone nearly 11.3 hours per day and watching TV 5.2 hours per day as I chose to do while writing this book.

FUN FACTS:

"American adults spend over 11 hours per day generally interacting with media." https://www.nielsen.com/us/en/insights/article/2018/time-flies-us-adults-now-spend-nearly-half-a-day-interacting-with-media/

"On average, American adults are watching five hours and four minutes of television per day." - https://www.nytimes.com/2016/07/01/business/media/nielsen-survey-media-viewing.html

---

It's hard to write a book when you feel as I do that it's my personal mission to interact with incoming barrage of social media updates, push notifications, text messages, phone calls, emails, and advertisements headed your way. In fact while writing this book I once spent nearly 4 hours defending my belief that President Obama was in fact in the United States of America and why 9.11 was an inside job organized by President Bush for "big oil." And now without any further ado, get ready for the literary laser show to begin.

Special Dedication:

This book is dedicated to myself, because I wrote it, and no one else did. To everyone on the team who helped me edit, typeset, and layout the book - don't get too excited, that's your job. To the humans on this planet, you are welcome, and enjoy!

AMERICA'S MOST HUMBLE MAN

P.S. A man did the artwork for this book, and I wanted to thank him for providing you these incredible illustrations, but I can't seem to recall his name.

THE PREAMBLE
(DRUM ROLL PLEASE)

THE MORE YOU TAKE OUT OF THIS BOOK,
THE LESS YOU WILL GET OUT OF LIFE

In order to help you to get the most of this book review the following:

1. As you read this book, stop and constantly ask yourself, how you are currently going about implementing these incredible tried and true, and proven tips for how to repel potential friends employees, customers, and how to not influence people.

2. You must develop a burning desire to hate money, and a maniacal commitment and obsession to not master the most profound principles of human relations.

3. Read each of the following chapters two times before choosing to scurry on to the next chapter.

4. When you find a super move that you are currently using to repel potential friends, employees and customers, invest the time to underscore each important idea and take additional time out of your schedule to celebrate the habits, traditions, and worldviews that are insuring that you are repelling people and having virtually no impact on the lives of others during the short amount of time that you are blessed to have on the planet earth.

5. Review this book each and every month to make sure that you are not doing anything that would cause you to win friends or influence people. You must stay loyal to dysfunction at all times. Whatever you've been doing that has kept you stuck at where you are at is something that you MUST KEEP DOING IF YOU WANT TO ACHIEVE THE SAME RESULTS.

6. Apply these principles whenever possible. Use these timeless principles to make small problems worse, to get offended whenever possible, and to make it difficult for productive people to get things done.

7. Make a fun game out of the implementation of the principles taught within this book. If you ever feel as though someone is not repelled by you or that you are beginning to influence people, take a moment and extend your middle finger at them. If they are still not offended, show them the ultimate super move for repelling potential friends, employees, customers, and stare in their direction while looking angry, simultaneously extending both of your middle fingers while pointing in their direction.

8. Check up on yourself each and every week to make sure that you are implementing the principles stated in this book so that you will ensure that you are living a life that repels everyone possible while guiding you down the path of making no positive influence or impact on the world around you.

9. Keep notes in the margins of this book so that you can remind yourself to stay focused, and loyal to any wealth-and-friend-repelling mindsets, habits, and communication styles you have.

10. As a bonus tip: Make sure that you only watch politically divisive news at all times, when debating both religion and politics with everyone who is near you, and smell bad at all times. Simply refuse to bathe daily. Have gross looking hair, and people will avoid you. Trust me, I know because once I went 17 weeks without bathing in order to write this book. At times, I actually began to hate myself.

How to Repel Potential Friends and Not Influence People

CHAPTER 1

IF YOU DON'T WANT TO GET HONEY AND YOU WANT TO GET STUNG, KICK OVER THE BEEHIVE

When you are out there attempting not to sell something to somebody, not trying to land a new client, and not become friends with someone, you must immediately find something that you disagree with them about and then you must obsess on it. If you are invited into their home, point out something and tell them "that's kind of tacky." If they mention that they just got back from church, tell them, "So you still believe in that?" I suppose you still believe in owning guns to protect yourself?" If they let that slide, and choose to turn the other cheek, get a running start and figuratively slap them in the other cheek. You must go out of your way to disagree on something if you want to truly learn *How to Repel Potential Friends, Employees & Customers & Not Influence People*.

Work hard at this, and just find something that they are not doing right in your mind's eye, and tell them as soon as possible with little, to no tact. You must find a place of disagreement and you must speak your mind at all times, if you want to ever achieve the goal of repelling potential friends, employees, and customers, and not influence people.

Attack the bee-hive again and again! I promise your body will get stung. When you do get stung act as though you are shocked as to why they would lash out at you. I live by this code, and it has allowed me to live on government subsidies in tent cities, in college dorm rooms, and in marijuana dispensaries for my entire adult life.

Continued, a practical example of how to put this plan into action. Years ago, I was dating a young lady, and things were going great. Now, this was before I started my quest to master the art of repelling potential friends, employees and customers, and not influence people. I believe I was 18 at the time, and her father invited me to go out to dinner with them at a very nice Chinese Buffet. The atmosphere was great. The overhead music was nice, and overall the ambiance was perfect.

Now the girl that I was dating was some denomination of the Baptist Christian Church. I grew up in an Assembly of God Church. Essentially, my girlfriend's family and my family agreed on 99% of our religious views. However, my family and her family did not agree on "speaking in tongues". For those of you out there who do not know what "speaking in tongues" means, YOU ARE A SINNER! It's where the person who has what is known as "the gift of tongues" is usually saying words that appear to be from a different language and a language, that the speaker does not understand. Experts call this phenomenon glossolalia, a Greek compound of the words glossa, meaning "tongue" or "language," and lalia, meaning "to talk." Anyway, the Assembly of God Church taught you actually want to pray for ability to "speak in tongues", and my girlfriend's father thought that speaking in tongues was an abomination, so our dinner that evening was ruined by the following exchange of words:

Kyle (My girlfriend's dad): "Claytron, we really appreciate you joining us for dinner tonight. What does your family normally do on a Sunday night?"

Claytron Menendez: "Well sir, we typically go to church on Sunday nights and Sunday mornings."

Kyle (My girlfriend's dad): "That's great, well thanks for being here."

Claytron Menendez: "Well, really I should thank my parents Tonight was of a big night for them."

Kyle (My girlfriend's dad): "Oh really, why?"

Claytron Menendez: "Well tonight was the night that my youth pastor was supposed to pray over me to receive the ability to "speak in tongues", and become an all-out holy roller!"

Kyle (My girlfriend's dad): "Well, we appreciate you. Thanks for sharing. Hey Deb, can you pass me an eggroll?"

Claytron Menendez: "Sir, I had a question."

Kyle (My girlfriend's dad): "Sure, what do you got?"

Claytron Menendez: "Why do ALL Baptists pick and choose the parts of the Bible that they want to believe in, sir?"

Kyle (My girlfriend's dad): "What are you talking about?"

Claytron Menendez: "Well, 1st Corinthians 14 states, "Follow the way of love and eagerly desire gifts of the Spirit, especially prophecy. For anyone who speaks in a tongue does not speak to people but to God. Indeed, no one understands them; they utter mysteries by the Spirit."

Kyle (My girlfriend's dad): "Well Claytron, I think we can all agree that we don't have to agree on everything, right?"

Claytron Menendez: "Well, if I'm going to marry your daughter, I just don't want her to burn in a fiery hell."

My girlfriend then kicked me in the shin from under the table, dinner ended quickly thereafter and so did our relationship.

The Epic Whale of a Tale Featuring America's Self-Proclaimed Most Humble Male

How to Repel Potential Friends and Not Influence People

CHAPTER 2

SURROUND YOURSELF WITH NEFARIOUS IDIOTS, DRAMATIC DUDES, FLAKY FRIENDS AND INVEST YOUR TIME TRYING TO CHANGE THEM

Although most of the world has accepted that the following statements are true, as the author of this incredible research-based book, I knew that I would have to suffer first-hand for you. As an investigative author, how can I possibly give you the very best tips for creating your worst life now, if I have not personally tested out my theories on *How to Repel Potential Friends and Not Influence People* myself? Read the following notable quotables out loud and emotionally, psychology and physically prepare yourself for what happened to me when I decided to surround myself exclusively with nafarrius idiots, dramatic dudes and flaky friends.

NOTABLE QUOTABLE

"You are the average of the five people you associate with most, so do not underestimate the effects of your pessimistic, unambitious, or disorganized friends. If someone isn't making you stronger, they're making you weaker."

TIM FERRISS

(The New York Times best-selling author of The 4-Hour Workweek (2007, expanded edition 2009), The 4-Hour Body (2010), The 4-Hour Chef (2012), Tools of Titans (2016), and Tribe of Mentors (2017), the podcaster and entrepreneur who has invested in or advised StumbleUpon, Posterous, Evernote, Shopify, etc.)

NOTABLE QUOTABLE

"The fastest way to change yourself is to hang out with people who are already the way you want to be."

REID HOFFMAN

(The American internet entrepreneur, venture capitalist and author. Hoffman was the co-founder and executive chairman of LinkedIn, a business-oriented social network used primarily for professional networking. He is currently a partner at the venture capital firm Greylock Partners. On the Forbes 2019 list of the world's billionaires, Hoffman was ranked #1349 with a net worth of US $1.8 billion)

"Walk with the wise and become wise, for a companion of fools suffers harm."

PROVERBS 13:20

(From that super controversial book known as The Bible)

In order to find nafarrius idiots, dramatic dudes, and flaky friends, and I did a quick Google search for the areas of town where the unholy gather. I combed Al Gore's internet for the places and spaces where vagrants voice their political opinions, where the vagabonds get their bail bonds, where high-interest cash advance loans are easy to come by, where liquor stores are prominent, and where pawn shop people are prone to be located. When I finally found my new home where I would begin testing my theories on how to repel potential friends, employees and customers and not influence people I almost cried. But, I didn't fear of looking weak in front of the gangbangers and the drug dealers.

Although most embedded investigative authors would have simply refused to move into a rough area of town to simply test their theories on how to repel potential friends, employers and customers, and not influence people, I'm frankly not an average author. I'm bold. I'm humble. I'm sexy. I'm Claytron Menendez.

So, I signed a lease in a run-down apartment complex with a front desk guy by the name of Randle. Randle had one-two, but it was a good one. Overwhelmed by how stressful the move had been on me psychologically, I had a hard time sleeping. Eventually, I fell asleep and was quickly awakened by car alarms going off outside. Around 2 AM, the alarms stopped going off, and then I heard what appeared to be gunshots. Aaround 4 AM, things had settled down, but now the smell of marijuana began flooding into my vents and the sound of what appeared to be giggling adults could be heard through the walls of my less-than well-maintained apartment. However, based on the fact that I wasn't smoking marijuana, I realized that my newfound neighbor might be having his apartment broken into by marijuana smokers!

Quickly, I knew that I had to do something, because nothing would be less than what was required. So, I sprang to my feet like a young Bruce Lee Puma-hybrid, and ran out of my apartment to potentially save the life of my new neighbor. In front of his apartment, things looked fishy. There was a 1982 Cadillac Coupe De Ville with custom rims parked out front. It had furry dice hanging from the mirror, and one of those air-freshers hanging down in the shape of a marijuana leaf. Maybe that was where the smell was coming from? Either way, as his new neighbor, I knew that it was my time to knock on his door, and make sure he was ok. So I first peered in the window and I could see three large men and women, who appeared to be wearing bathing suits. I found this to be odd, as it was December during this moment in time, and the community pool was closed. In fact, come to think about it, the pool was actually empty, and spray-painted with uplifting messages such as "For a Good Time Call Sherrie Wells", and "F$#% the Police." Well, if I was going to check on my neighbor, I knew that the time was never going to be just right, and that my time was now. So, I knocked on the door three times and then I immediately heard a voice yell out from behind the door, "Lil' Mookie is that you?! Cuz...Lil' Mookie is that you!"

I responded, "No sir, this is not Little Mookie. This is Claytron Menendez, your new neighbor, and I came by to check to see if you were ok. Before I reported anything to police, I wanted to make sure you were okay, and that pot smoking robbers were not robbing you and leaving you with the smell of marijuana in your home. Are you ok?!"

The door immediately opened. I don't remember what came next, but I woke up in a local hospital with a fractured skull, two black eyes, an odd, foggy memory of three men yelling, "Beat his a#%!" I hope they found the robber who beat me up.

It's a shame, however, but due to my extensive injuries I never was able to really invest the time needed to determine if there was any truth to my hypothesis that if you surround yourself with nefarious idiots, dramatic dudes, criminal minds and flaky friends, that your quality of life will go down.

How to Repel Potential Friends and Not Influence People

CHAPTER 3

HE WHO CAN REPEL EVERYONE IS EMPOWERED TO SPRINT NAKED THROUGH THE TOLL ROAD OF LIFE

Over these past nine years, I have been "over-qualified" for most jobs and "under-employed" by any standard. However, my personal devotion and commitment to testing my theories on *How to Repel Potential Friends and Not Influence People* has never waivered. Because our welfare system is so strong, I can still afford to eat and attend college. I actually just completed my degrees from the University of Phoenix in the fields of History, Eastern European Art, and American films. But I think I want to go back to school to earn my Master's of Divinity. That's what I need to really separate my resume from the pack.

Anyway, during my studies, I have discovered that all successful people try to find a problem that they can solve for others and they essentially strive to add value to everyone they come in contact with. Thus, I've decided to focus exclusively on what I want, and talk in third person when possible. It's been truly amazing to me how little people care about "Claytron Menendez", and his ideas now. When "Claytron Menendez" is around others, his dedication to this method of repelling potential friends and employees is spectacular.

In fact eleven years and four days ago, "Claytron Menendez" (I) was invited to interview for the position of assistant to the Vice President of a small regional bank. During my job interview with the middle-aged balding man who had the potential to be my future boss, our interview went like this:

Bald Potential Boss: "Claytron, my name is Douglas Smith and I'm the Vice President of Southern Valley River Bank. What makes you qualified for the job?"

Me: "Well Mr. Clean, I'm really more interested in how much you can pay me."

Douglas Smith: "Claytron, why did you just call me Mr. Clean?"

Me: "Well, because you are bald...and you...you look like Mr. Clean from the neck up."

Douglas Smith: "Well Claytron, I kind of find that to be a little offensive, but I'm willing to look past that. So tell me what makes you qualified for the job?"

Me: "Mr. Douglas "Clean" I think that you are failing to see the potential talent you have in front of you. I hold degrees from the University of Phoenix in the fields of History, Eastern European Art, and American films. Just answer my question. As your assistant, how much cash am I going to be raking in?"

I did not get the job.

The Epic Whale of a Tale Featuring America's Self-Proclaimed Most Humble Male

How to Repel Potential Friends and Not Influence People

CHAPTER 4

PROVIDE FEEDBACK AND CRITICISM TO PEOPLE WHO AREN'T ASKING FOR YOUR ADVICE

During the past years, I have sacrificed my life, my career, and my good looks for your benefit, and for the testing of my theories of *How to Repel Potential Friends and Not Influence People*. Much to my non-surprise (because I know everything already), I have discovered that when you provide feedback and criticism to people who aren't asking for your advice, it angers them. So here's a quick note to all of the husbands out there. Do you want to irritate your wife? Here's a pro tip. If you want to irritate your wife, tell her what she is not doing well when she is not asking for your feedback. And to the ladies out there (by the way, it's ladies night every night in the world of Claytron Menendez) make sure that you go out of your way to provide feedback, constructive criticism, and opinions to your husband even when he's not asking for it so that you can guarantee that you will repel him and not influence him.

One day, just to test my theories on the power of providing unsolicited feedback, advice and criticism to people who are not seeking it from you, I joined a big box fitness center for around 10 bucks per month. Much to my shocked amazement and enjoyment, the night I joined the gym, was the night of their pizza party. So, I ate pizza, and ALOT of pizza. I'm talking about devouring entire boxes of pizza. At a certain point, I felt physical pain. The entire time I was eating, I noticed that the women were looking at me with a look of disgust, which I returned with a wink. Shortly after downing four boxes of pizza, seven breadsticks, and without washing my hands, I knew it was time to make my move. So I went for it.

I walked up to the yoga-pant-wearing, "soccer mom" looking lady in her mid-thirties who I had just winked at moments earlier. However, she was no longer staring at me in obvious amazement as I crushed those pizzas. No, she was now working out, and she was working out like Jillian Michaels in her workout DVD series, *Shred-It with Weights Levels 1 & 2*. Honestly, I didn't really care for volumes 3 & 4. Anyway, the point was, this lady was aggressively working out on a thigh machine that she was using to sculpt her thighs by aggressively pushing her thighs in and out. Now, being the kind of man that I am, I didn't want to interrupt her workout, so I just attentively invested ten minutes of my time to gaze at her and watch her complete twelve sets of 12 reps. Oh, and I counted each and every repetition to myself and then I said these words, "Excuse me, ma'am. I couldn't help but notice that you just did 12 sets of 12 reps. However, during *Shred-It with Weights Levels 1 & 2*, Jillian Michaels recommends doing less sets. Don't you think you might be overdoing it? If your thighs get too tight, you may end up being a venus flytrap where you..."

I got slapped.

The Epic Whale of a Tale Featuring America's Self-Proclaimed Most Humble Male

How to Repel Potential Friends and Not Influence People

CHAPTER 5

DO THIS AND YOU'LL MAKE PEOPLE HATE YOU

If you want to guarantee yourself that you will know *How to Repel Potential Friends and Not Influence People*, you must make sure that you never appear interested in your fellow man, regardless of how much they deserve or need your attention. Furthermore, if you want to repel humans on the planet Earth, make sure that you never greet other people with enthusiasm or animation. Make sure that you always sound somewhere between tired, bored, distracted, and "happy to be ending your shift" when people call. When you demonstrate a sincere disinterest in other people, you will develop the type of disloyalty to yourself and your company that makes poverty possible.

I once landed a job at a sandwich shop with brick wallpaper that lets you choose your favorite color of bread, meat, veggies and all of that kind of crap. I will never forget my first (and last day) on the job. I arrived four minutes late to my shift (hey, there was traffic) with my uniform looking like I had left it in the car over a rainy weekend, while forgetting to roll up the windows of my car (which is exactly what happened) My boss said in the nicest and kindest tone, "Claytron, are you okay? And, what's going on with your uniform?" I simply looked down at my shoes and said, "Whatev."

My wonderfully cheerful, middle-aged boss said, "Well Claytron here at our sandwich shop, we believe that arriving 15 minutes early is on-time."

And then, I yawned because I was still tired from all the video-gaming from the night before, and then it occured to me. OH NO! - I forgot to call the girl I met at the club last night to wake her up for her shift at Wal-Mart. While looking at my phone and intensely typing a text message to my "boo", I said with little to no focused energy, "So am I gonna get paid for that?"

I got fired.

The Epic Whale of a Tale Featuring America's Self-Proclaimed Most Humble Male

How to Repel Potential Friends and Not Influence People

CHAPTER 6

A GREAT WAY TO A BAD FIRST IMPRESSION

I have found during my short thirty five years on the planet, that opportunities are everywhere and the only true way to avoid them all, is to smell bad, to scowl, and look universally annoyed at anybody, every time they ask me a question about anything. Oh, this method works like a charm. Whereas a fat little three-month-old baby and a bulldog puppy attracts the interest of everyone, I've found that when you look angry at all times, people will pay you no mind. It's my move.

I once landed a job as a waiter at a restaurant that was desperate for a "warm body", which meant that I was the right guy for this job. So, two hours before my shift, I bathed in the most potent cat pee that I could find and then I put on my work uniform and arrived in the parking lot thirty minutes before my shift. When I walked in and shook that hand of my manager for that first day of work...MAN you should have seen the look on her face. She said, "Oh my! What is that smell!" I quickly chimed in. "Ma'am, that smell is me. I bathed in cat pee just before work today. It's just a cultural and religious ritual that I'm into."

I got fired.

How to Repel Potential Friends and Not Influence People

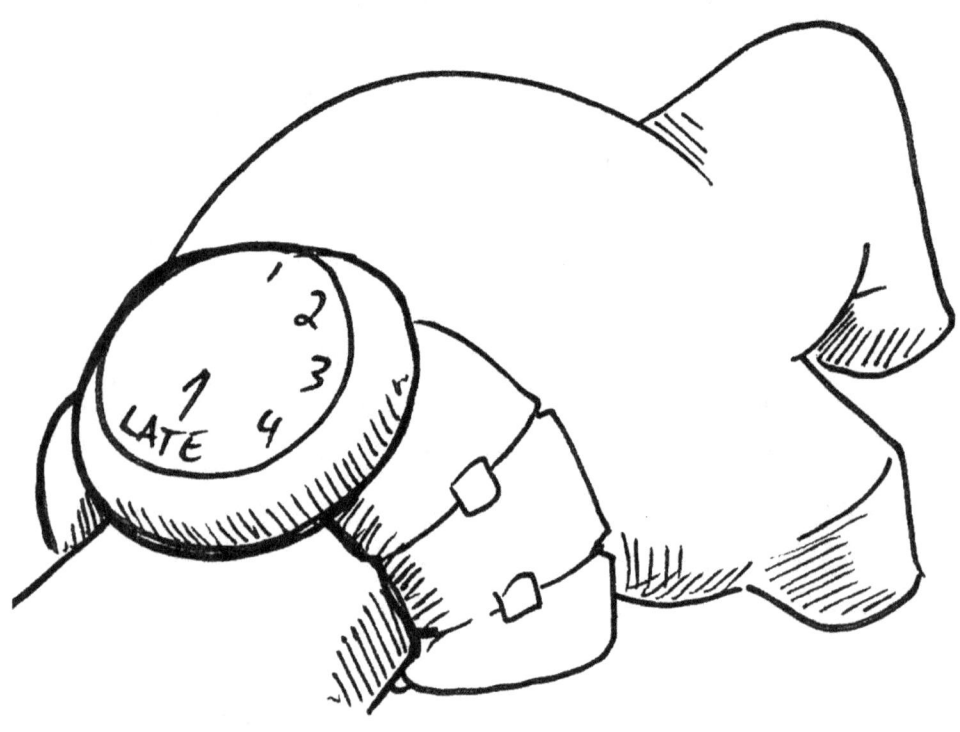

CHAPTER 7

ABL – ALWAYS BE LATE (AND ALWAYS HAVE AN EXCUSE THAT YOU BELIEVE FOR BEING LATE)

NOTABLE QUOTABLE

"A man has no right to occupy another man's time unnecessarily."

JOHN D. ROCKEFELLER

(The world's most wealthy man who began working at the age of 13)

My research into *How to Repel Potential Friends and Not Influence People* has shown me time and time again that a super move that will cause you to lose all rapport, trust, and respect from everyone, is to be late, and to always have an excuse that you actually believe for being late. However, according to Inc. Magazine, "A hefty 15 to 20 percent of U.S. workers are late to the job on a regular basis." So, I really wanted to invest the time needed to advance my noble cause, and to help out somewhere between 80% and 85% of the Americans who are committed to losing at all costs. Thus, I wanted to use the scientific method to prove once and for all, that being late will in fact cause you to lose all rapport, trust, and respect from everyone. So, here is what I did for you:

FUN FACT

"A hefty 15 to 20 percent of U.S. workers are late to the job on a regular basis."

- https://www.inc.com/kenny-kline/tardiness-costs-american-economy-a-shocking-amount-of-money-each-year.html

---

First off, I have never worked harder and more diligently, than I did to prove that being late is a pro tip for never being promoted or trusted by anybody with a sound mind. I landed a job at a local ice cream store / restaurant / grocery store as a clerk, and I showed up early by 30 minute every day for 4 months in a row. I never missed a day of work. I never broke a single rule. I simply did what I was told with cheerful enthusiasm, and then one day, it happened and I knew it would. I got asked to become the manager of the local ice cream store / restaurant / grocery store. That's when I took off my mask.

Day one as a manager, I vowed to fall on the sword for this project, and for my research to teach the world *How to Repel Potential Friends and Not Influence People*, my alarm went off at 6 AM, like it had each and every day for the past four months in a row, but, when it went off, I passionately hit the snooze button four times. And then I continued to slumber and sleep like never before. Like a bear in hibernation, I forced myself to sleep, and then I arrived to work my shift at 9:14 AM, when I was supposed to be there at 9:00 AM.

Right away, I could sense that the twelve employees underneath me were not a fan of me being late, so I threw out a believable reason for being late. I said, "Guys I apologize for being late. I had a car problem on the way to work."

Richard (The Assistant Manager): "Well, I used to work at a repair shop. Let me look at it and I'll fix it. You drive a Chevy right?"

Claytron Menendez: "When I was driving, it made this sound like BOOM-CHICK-BOOM-WAP-WAP-BANG-BANG and I was like NO! Then the check engine light went on and I knew I had to pull over to make sure that I was being responsible for the health of my vehicle. But all is well now."

Richard (The Assistant Manager): "Well, Mr. Claytron I'm actually a Chevy-certified specialist and I still own the diagnostic equipment that I can just plug into your car and it will show me a digital print out of any of the check engine light warnings that have ever shown up during your vehicle's history."

Claytron Menendez: "You know Richard. I appreciate you, but my uncle is actually a Chevy-certified specialist and he has already told me that he will look at it."

Richard (The Assistant Manager): "Really! Cool, I actually used to be a volunteer for the Chevy-certified specialists in America, so I still have a list of all of the current members. I'll look him up after work and give him a call. I love connecting with Chevy-certified specialists. We are kind of a fraternity.

Once Chevy, always Chevy. What's his name?"

Claytron Menendez: "Ummm...well I cannot disclose this at the time as he is in hiding right now due to a recent court case that he is involved in."

Richard (The Assistant Manager): "But, I thought you said that he was going to help you fix your vehicle?"

Claytron Menendez: "He is. But he's going to fix my vehicle during the dark of night, when the world can't see him, and he's able to hide his face."

I willed myself to be late for four more days in a row and then an all out mutiny broke out, and I was fired. I am still scarred by the very thought of the emotional pain that I went through. But I did find that when you are perpetually late, people really do begin to hate you.

The Epic Whale of a Tale Featuring America's Self-Proclaimed Most Humble Male

How to Repel Potential Friends and Not Influence People

CHAPTER 8

IF YOU DO THIS MOVE YOU WILL CERTAINLY BE ON A COLLISION COURSE WITH FAILURE.

If you want to make sure that you become a master of *How to Repel Potential Friends and Not Influence People*, you want to make sure that you never call someone by their first name, and go out of your way to never learn it.

About seven years ago, I landed a job working in a toll booth for the State of Oklahoma's Turnpike Authority, and my supervisor's name was Michael. During the first weekly team meeting when all forty-two members of the staff were gathered, I asked for permission to address the team with a quick win of the week. After permission was granted by Michael, I invested five minutes of the meeting to praise my boss for how hard he worked, and what a great example he was setting for our entire team. And then I ended my words of encouragement by saying, "Now let's all raise a glass of coffee to celebrate Mark!".

All of sudden things got awkward and people began to mumble, whisper, and chatter. The meeting ended with awkwardly with Michael immediately approaching me to say,

"Claytron, I really do appreciate the work you do and for the kind words. However, I also wanted to remind you that my name is Michael, and not Mark."

I responded with, "No problem Mark. I mean, no problem Michael."

Michael: "Ok. I appreciate you working hard. Just remember my name is Michael."

In the following weeks I intentionally referred to Michael as, "Mitch, Martin, Maurice, Trevor, Karl, Mack and Buddy. Each time he corrected me, Michael grew more and more angry and I acted as though I was sincerely sorry, and just accidentally forgot."

After three consecutive weeks of calling Michael by the wrong name, I was told that they no longer had enough hours for me to justify keeping me employed there.

The Epic Whale of a Tale Featuring America's Self-Proclaimed Most Humble Male

CHAPTER 9

A SUPER-MOVE TO BECOME A DULL CONVERSATIONALIST

When you listen intently to what people are saying when they talk to you, they love it. When people sense that you are genuinely interested in them and what they are saying, they love it. In fact, attentively listening is one of the highest forms of compliments that you can ever really show somebody. When you focus 100% of your interest and attention on the person that is speaking to you, people love it. However, this book is about my great quest to teach you *How to Repel Potential Friends and Not Influence People*, and so an example may be needed here.

When you find yourself in a team meeting, attempting to have a sincere conversation, attending church, or out to date with your significant other, make sure that you bring your phone with you on the date and invest at least 80% of the date to glancing at your phone, interacting with it, and taking the action steps that you need to take to let the other person know that they are simply a distraction from your main focus, and the source of "the real action" known as your smartphone.

Years ago, because of my extensive background in working with sound systems, I was asked by my local church to see if I could help to run the soundboard and mixer for the church once per month. I said yes. However, to test my hypothesis on how to become a super-dull conversationalist, I made sure that anytime that the Pastor attempted to speak to me, I would promptly inform him that, "Oh. I'm sorry.

I've got to take this call."

In fact, during one service as he was waving at me desperately to unmute his microphone I waved him off and mouthed to him that I had to take the inbound call that was coming in because it was coming in from "long distance."

The Epic Whale of a Tale Featuring America's Self-Proclaimed Most Humble Male

How to Repel Potential Friends and Not Influence People

CHAPTER 10

HOW TO GUARANTEE THAT PEOPLE INSTANTLY DON'T LIKE YOU

We all instinctively know that people's favorite topic is themselves, yet we so rarely invest the time needed to research the things liked by the person that is coming to visit us, or that we have a scheduled meeting with. If you want to get people to become interested in you, you must first become interested in them because people's favorite topic is themselves.

However, if you want to guarantee that people instantly don't like you, never take the time needed to learn about them and the things that they are interested in. In fact, this reminds me of a story that took place a long-time ago, perhaps up to four days ago.

Four days ago, I received an invitation from someone that my brother ,Clay Clark, knows how to raise money for the preservation of the local Rose Garden and Museum. Honestly to me nothing could be more boring and soul-sucking that to have to invest both the time and money needed to raise funding for the Garden Center. As a man who has devoted nearly a decade of his life to learning just *How to Repel Potential Friends, Employees & Customers & to Not Influence People*, I felt that it would be a great social experiment to see how long I could carry on a conversation with a person, if I refused to care at all about anything that they were saying. My first test was with the head of the Garden Center who approached me to say "hello", and to make sure that I wasn't a protester or something the moment his eyes first saw that my black t-shirt had the following statement printed on it with white letters, "Don't Talk to Me!"

Randall Gustuphson (The Head of the Rose Garden): "Excuse me sir, but may we have a word?"

Claytron Menendez: "Sure, but what word? Ha, ha, ha?"

Randall Gustuphson (The Head of the Rose Garden): "Sir what brings you out to support the Garden Center."

Claytron Menendez: "Randall, I'm not sure what you just said, but are you serving barbecue tonight?"

Randall Gustuphson (The Head of the Rose Garden): "Sir, I said what brings you to support the Garden Center?"

Claytron Menendez: "Yes, yes…but where are the cheese cubes and the crackers?"

Randall Gustuphson (The Head of the Rose Garden): "Sir, I'm not quite sure how we are miscommunicating, but what brings you to support the Garden Center?"

Claytron Menendez: "Randall, you remind me of my cousin's wife."

Shortly after I was asked to leave.

The Epic Whale of a Tale Featuring America's Self-Proclaimed Most Humble Male

How to Repel Potential Friends and Not Influence People

CHAPTER 11

EMAIL PEOPLE CONSTANTLY

Poor people believe that you can always create more time, and that you cannot create more money. Thus, I will tell you that the best way *How to Repel Potential Friends and Not Influence People,* is to make sure that you email your employees, friends and customers constantly. If you are 100% committed to really learning how to *How to Repel Potential Friends and Not Influence People,* you must learn to communicate via email only so that you can:

1. Hide behind your keyboard and write bold things that you would never actually say to the person you are emailing.

2. Overwhelm people each and every morning with an avalanche of unnecessary memos, quotes, and newsletters to read.

3. Irritate people by filling up their inbox with your random epiphanies, Chuck Norris Jokes, and time-wasting updates.

How to Repel Potential Friends and Not Influence People

CHAPTER 12

YOU CAN WIN AN ARGUMENT IF YOU YELL LOUD ENOUGH

The legendary author of **How to Win Friends and Influence People**, Dale Carnegie once wrote, "You can't win an argument" and that "I have come to the conclusion that there is only one way under high heaven to get the best of an argument— and that is to avoid it." However, I can tell you this:

If you want to really know how to *How to Repel Potential Friends and Not Influence People*, I recommend that you invest your time in arguing with socialists about unsolvable arguments such as, why socialists are wrong about how economies work and why Israel is right and Palestine is wrong 100% of the time.

How to Repel Potential Friends and Not Influence People

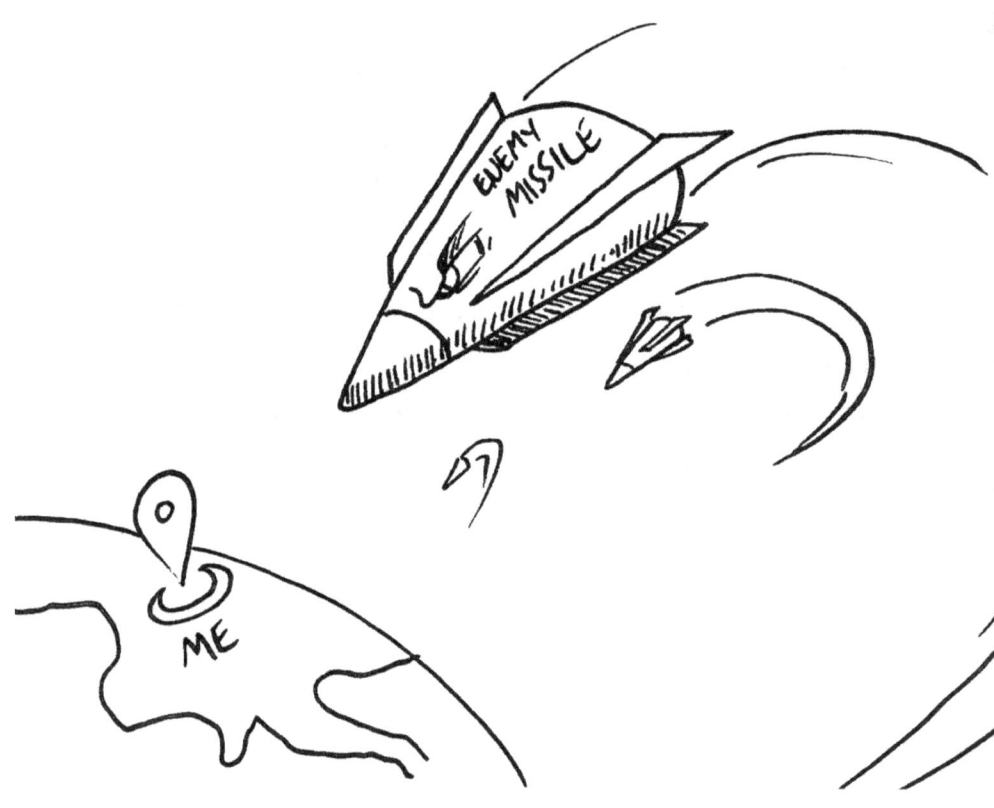

CHAPTER 13

THE BEST WAY TO MAKE AN ENEMY AND HOW TO MAKE ENEMY CREATION UNAVOIDABLE AT ALL TIMES

If you want people to dislike you from the very first interaction that you have with them, you must commit yourself to telling them, "you are wrong" at some point during your next conversation. Sure you can let people know that they are wrong with a look or a gesture, but you must simply not come out and say that "you are wrong" to most people most of the time to make them REALLY mad.

Many moons ago, I was hired to work at a local organic grocery store in the produce section. Each day, the vast majority of the customers were nice and courteous to me because I was nice to them and because our store provided our ideal and likely buyers with the organic produce that was hard to find anywhere else. However, every once in awhile, a customer would attempt to rattle my cage by asking me over and over in different ways, why organic produce costs two to three times more than regular produce. Here are the words that got me fired from the job:

Claytron Menendez: "Sir, is there anything that I can help you with?"

Customer: "No, I'm good. I'm just so irritated that your food costs three times more than it costs just a mile away over at Sprouts. Why do you price your organic food so high?"

Claytron Menendez: "Sir, that's a great question, and one that I often asked myself before I started here. But, essentially, organic produce is not filled with all of the chemicals, hormones, and pesticides. So, the quality and the nutritional value of organic produce is significantly higher than that of non-organic food."

Customer: "I get it, but it is three times more money than regular produce. I mean, non-organic food can't be that bad can it?"

Claytron Menendez: "Sir you are a great person, but you are 100% wrong."

As soon as I told the customer that they were wrong, they grew hostile and began to ask to speak to a manager because of my attitude. Soon thereafter, I was fired, after telling my 14th customer that they were wrong during the first thirty days of my employment.

The Epic Whale of a Tale Featuring America's Self-Proclaimed Most Humble Male

CHAPTER 14

GET AS MANY REGRETTABLE TATTOOS AS POSSIBLE WHILE ANGRY, DEPRESSED, DRUNK OR HIGH

We've all had bad things happen to us, and if you haven't had a bad thing happen to you, just wait...it will happen. However, if you want to make sure that people ask about the no-good-very-bad-and-rotten thing that happened to you, make sure that you memorialize and pay tribute to the bad thing that happened to you by getting a tattoo on your forearm so that you can forever be asked about the bad thing that happened to you by everyone whom you just met. In fact, as a tip for *How to Repel Potential Friends and Not Influence People*, I recommend that you only get tattoos when you are angry, depressed, drunk or high. And by doing this, you will ensure that even the people you just met while serving drinks at a bartender at your local tavern will be concerned about your sanity and overall mental health.

In fact, if you are looking for a good role model of what you should do in terms of tattoos to *Repel Potential Friends and Not Influence People*, just do a quick search for Post Malone and Aaron Carter, and do what they're doing without having the fan bases that they have. However, to insure that the burden of being successful is never in your future, you want to make sure that you get your facial tattoos way before you begin to gain traction with your career in music or any other industry.

Recently, to prepare for the writing of this book I went out and got Post Malone's facial tattoos temporarily replicated on my face and I applied for any entry level job that I could find to work as a clerk, warehouse employee, barista, waiter or greeter. And guess what? Nobody called me back after they saw my face. Why? Because potential employers seemed to be worried about my emotional state. Did I feel discriminated against? Yes. How dare potential employers not hire me because my face would not make a favorable first impression to their ideal and likely buyers? How dare they judge me. In fact, I now judge the potential employers who rejected me (while living with my mother again at the age of 32).

The Epic Whale of a Tale Featuring America's Self-Proclaimed Most Humble Male

CHAPTER 15

A SPOONFUL OF DRANO MAKES THE MEDICINE GO DOWN

President Woodrow Wilson once wrote, "If you come at me with your fists doubled I think I can promise you that mine will double as fast as yours. But, if you come to me and say, let us sit down and take counsel together and if we differ from each other, understand why it is that we differ, just what the points are at issue are, we will presently find that we are not so far apart after all, that the points on which we differ are few and the points on which we agree are many, and that if we only have the patience and the candor and the desire to get together, we will get together."

However, what you must learn if you are truly learning to master your craft of learning *How to Repel Potential Friends and Not Influence People* is that you must come at people with double fists if you want to ensure that you receive an unreasonable and aggressive response from each and every one of your adversaries.

We all remember the musical where Mary Poppins once sang, "Just a spoonful of sugar makes the medicine go down." Well, I have an entirely different approach to dealing with adversity. When I need the other party to put my medicine down their throat, I like to say "Just a spoonful of Drano makes the medicine go down", because this poison will have terrible and horrible effects on the human body including damaging your opposition's esophagus, and stomach for several weeks. And then death will usually occur several months later.

The Epic Whale of a Tale Featuring America's Self-Proclaimed Most Humble Male

How to Repel Potential Friends and Not Influence People

CHAPTER 16

PET A CAT BACKWARDS AND NAME IT "SH@# HEAD"

Suppose that you are managing a large group of people, and you begin to notice that one of your long-time key employees is now struggling to deliver his projects on time and on budget. Do you fire this member of your team? No. Unless you are trying to diligently learn *How to Repel Potential Friends and Not Influence People*. In fact, if you were trying to win friends and influence people, you would call for a private meeting with one of your employees, and you would say something to the effect of: "Karl, you have been an incredible asset of our company over the past fifteen years, and you have never missed deadlines. Last week you missed two of them. What happened?"

By doing this, you give Karl a chance to self-reflect in front of an audience of one, and you allow him to save face in front of his teammates and co-workers.

However, if you want to make sure that you are mastering *How to Repel Potential Friends and Not Influence People*, you are going to want to call Karl out in front of his teammates, and you are going to make him feel so bad that he quits his job because the shame of having even missed one deadline ever, in the history of his tenure with you, is too much to bear. That my friend is a textbook super-move for *How to Repel Potential Friends, Employees & Customers & to Not Influence People*. Calling Karl out in public after making one mistake, is the equivalent of naming your family's favorite cat, "Sh$% Head", and petting your cat backwards as you attempt to pet the cat that you haven't attempted to pet once during the past three years.

The Epic Whale of a Tale Featuring America's Self-Proclaimed Most Humble Male

How to Repel Potential Friends and Not Influence People

CHAPTER 17

NO MATTER WHAT JUST HAPPENED, ONE UP EVERYBODY IN THEIR MOMENT OF TRIUMPH

One key that I have found for repelling potential friends, employees and customers, is to become obsessed with one-upping them at every opportunity. If one of your employees is having a baby, make sure to steal their thunder and dwell on the time when you and your wife first celebrated your baby's birth.

When someone brags about their baby and shares with you when their baby first learned to walk, make sure that you tell them your baby learned to walk faster (regardless of whether that is true or not). The key to one-ups-manship is to always turn the focus on the moment and the room on yourself at all times, so that no one else can ever experience great things other than you within your organization. And if you do this consistently enough, I can tell you that this move is a great lesson on *How to Repel Potential Friends and Not Influence People.*

How to Repel Potential Friends and Not Influence People

CHAPTER 18

THE GASOLINE YOU CAN POUR ON THE FIRES OF COMPLAINTS

When a customer or person is upset about something, it is best to let them vent and implement the B.L.A.S.T. strategy if you are trying to win friends and influence people. In fact, both Yum! Brands, Inc. (Kentucky Fried Chicken, Taco Bell, Pizza Hut, Wingstreet worldwide) and Chick-fil-A both teach their employees variations of the following methodology and strategy for dealing with customer complaints:

B - Believe what the person is saying, or at least deeply attempt to have the perspective that you believe, that they are sincerely frustrated, and that you are focused on helping them solve their legitimate problem.

L - Listen to what the other person is saying until they have let out their hot air, until they have vented their frustrations, and until they have talked themselves off the ledge.

A - Answer their issue with some type of proposed solution that is a win-win for both parties.

S - Satisfaction for both parties is what you are seeking here. So see if the win-win solution that you have proposed for both parties truly satisfies the upset party.

T - Trust is the ultimate goal here. You want to make sure that most parties trust each other when all is said and done. Document the agreement that both parties came to, and agree on a timeline for when the situation will be resolved (when the problem will be fixed, when the refund will be issued, etc.).

However, I view myself as a research martyr when it comes to gathering enough solid data on truly *How to Repel Potential Friends and Not Influence People* and so about three years ago, I took a job at a fast food mexican restaurant so that I could test my theories on the blasty-blast situations that would be created if I implemented the B.L.A.S.T. system in reverse, and the results were amazing.

A kind man in his 40's driving a minivan that was filled with three girls and his wife, pulled up to the window to get his order of six bean soft tacos, six beverages, an order of nachos, and six containers of fresh salsa. I took payment from him and then I gave him a tied plastic bag (so that he couldn't immediately see what was in the bag) filled with four soft tacos, six beverages, an order of guacamole and seven containers of fresh salsa. I told him thank you for his order, he thanked me and then away he went. twelve minutes later he pulled up to the drive through window and calmly stated, "Sir, yes I ordered six bean soft tacos, 6 beverages, an order of nachos and six containers of fresh salsa, and I did not get the right order. Can I exchange this? We haven't touched any of the food, but it's all wet."

Knowing deep in my heart that this was a nice man who was just trying to get the food he ordered for his family, I thought about doing the right thing, but then I remembered, I was doing the right thing in the long-term. I had to stay focused on my research, and I needed more hard data on *How to Repel Potential Friends and Not Influence People* and so I said:

Believe - "Sir I believe you are incorrect, but nice try guy."

The man said, "Hey pal, I'm not trying to have any problems here, I'm just trying to get the food I ordered."

Listen - Then I said, "Sir, listen here. I've been working as the drive through guy for several weeks and I can tell when somebody is trying to scam us. Stand down, and take the food we gave you or you might have to see my angry side, and you don't want to see my angry side. It's mad, angry, and really not pleasant. Sir, it's time to move on and let it go. Put it in the past. Sir, you have got to move on and now you are holding up the line."

The man then said, "Listen here pal, I'm tired of your crap."

The man's wife interrupted, "Honey, it's not worth it, just it go."

Then I said, "Sir, oh it's worth fighting for those six bean soft tacos, six beverages, an order of nachos and six containers of fresh salsa. Come on and bring it buddy!"

The man yelled, "Honey, I can't let this piece of sh$% talk to me that way. Let me deal with him."

At this point his young daughters in the back of his minivan were crying and for a moment I felt bad about my research, but I pressed on.

Answer - "Sir, I have answered your questions to the best of my abilities and I am frankly tired of watching you make young girls cry. If you don't move your vehicle out of this drive-thru line, I'm going to have to call the cops."

The man then screamed with veins bulging out his head, "I'm going to have your job. What is your name? I'm going to call your manager and get you fired!"

Satisfy - I then said, "My name is satisfied and that is what I am. I am satisfied that you got your six bean soft tacos, six beverages, an order of nachos and six containers of fresh salsa and now you must move on dude!"

The man then said, "I can't believe this crap, what is wrong with you!?"

Trust - I then looked at him like how a vulture looks into the eyes of a dead deer that he is about to devour and said, "Sir, you can trust me on this. I hope you and your six bean soft tacos, six beverages, an order of nachos and six containers of fresh salsa have a nice day!"

The man drove off and after my boss listened to the audio recording of my interaction with the customer, I was subsequently fired for "adding more fuel to the fire."

The Epic Whale of a Tale Featuring America's Self-Proclaimed Most Humble Male

How to Repel Potential Friends and Not Influence People

CHAPTER 19

MAKE PROBLEMS SEEM UNFIXABLE AND DWELL ON THEM WITHOUT TRYING TO SOLVE THEM

The adversity quotient is a score that measures your ability to quickly deal with adversities in your life and the term was actually coined by The *Thrivetime Show Podcast* guest and best-selling author of the *Adversity Quotient: Turning Obstacles into Opportunities*, Paul Stoltz, and ALL successful people would advise you that we all gain strength through struggle, and that you must learn from your failures and rejections and then quickly move on as soon as possible. So, when you get cut off in traffic, successful people would advise you to get over it immediately, and when you get hung up on while cold calling, successful people would advise you to get over the guaranteed rejections that you will face immediately.

However, in my passionate attempt to learn the dark art of *How to Repel Potential Friends and Not Influence People*, I have committed nearing a decade of my life to lamenting over everything including even the smallest rejections for days, weeks, months, and years. As examples:

Once, when someone forgot to introduce me to another person during a dinner situation, I stayed upset about it for seven complete days.

When people don't return my calls, I immediately question the solidness of our relationship and obsess about what caused the deterioration of our bond without stopping to think, maybe they just don't return anyone's calls.

When I go out to dinner, if the food is not exactly how I like it, I will not eat it, and then I will look angry for eight solid hours after the meal.

When somebody forgets a small detail that we talked about, I accuse them of not liking me, not paying attention to me, and not caring about our relationship.

When people violate their agreements with me, I stew on it for days and months, and spend thousands of dollars on legal fees.

When anything is not right, I will fight.

No slight or negative comment on social media is too small for me to lament on. I have simply chosen to spend the last decade of my life refusing to move on. As a result of it, I have gone nowhere and I have achieved nothing other than the writing of this incredible manuscript. You're welcome.

The Epic Whale of a Tale Featuring America's Self-Proclaimed Most Humble Male

How to Repel Potential Friends and Not Influence People

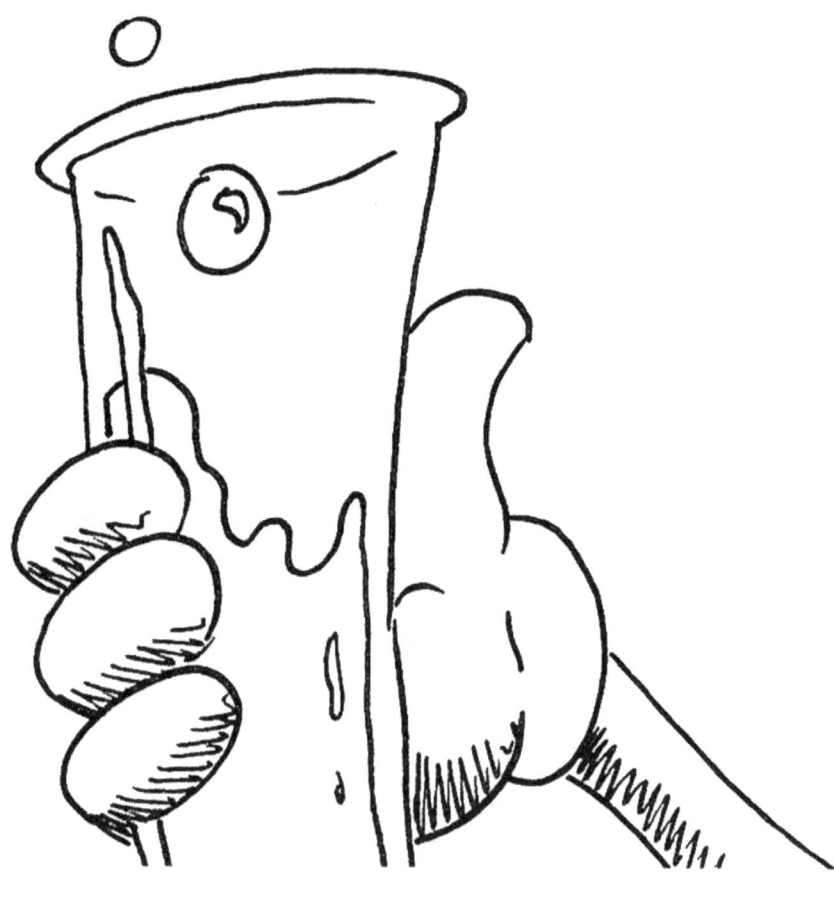

CHAPTER 20

THE MAGICAL FORMULA THAT WILL CAUSE EVEN SWEET ELDERLY CHRISTIAN WOMEN TO GIVE YOU "THE FINGER."

If you want to win friends and influence people, you must remember that many people on the planet earth are simultaneously sincere, and yet wrong about a great many things and thus, you don't want to condemn those that are wrong. Instead, you want to take the time needed to attempt to understand them because only wise people do that kind of thing.

If you want to go down the path of trying to win friends and influence people, it is wise to constantly ask yourself, "How would I actually feel if I too shared those same life experiences and were in their shoes?" In fact, I would argue that your ability to build relationships, to win friends and influence people depends heavily on your ability to see the world from the other person's point of view.

However, in order to gather the necessary data, I needed to craft this fabulous and majestic manuscript about *How To Repel Potential Friends And Not Influence People*. I have committed myself to acting as though I cannot understand anyone's point of view for over a decade.

In fact, once upon a time, I landed a job working at a retirement facility with elderly people just so that I could test my theories. After applying for many retirement facilities, I eventually landed a job as a "home health aid and activities coordinator" for a low-cost retirement home who had recently laid off their talented people for budgetary reasons, and I was their "Plan B."

During my first night on the job I was tasked with leading the community's weekly Bingo game, and I was the official Bingo caller for a crowd of approximately twenty five senior citizens who on average were in their late 70s. After explaining all of the rules and what prizes we had to give away, I made my first call of the night.

I said, "B 33, again that's B 33."

At that moment, a sweet elderly woman who appeared to be in her early 80's said, "I'm sorry. I can't hear you. Can you please repeat that call sir?"

And with the thought in mind that this wasn't going to go well I calmly yelled back, "Mam. Ignorance is no excuse, you must pay better attention lady!"

The crowd was shocked. Next I called, "I 44 Again that is I 44."

Quickly, a man who appeared to be at least 90, raised his hand. And I said, "Sir, I can't hear you. We can't hear the words you are saying. Our last "Bingo Caller" used to use a microphone to help us hear what he was saying. We would really appreciate it if you could use the microphone that is mounted on your podium. Thank you son. I really do appreciate you."

Then, with the goal in mind of gathering objective data for this book, I said, "Sir, I can hear everything just fine. Why don't you pay more attention?"

At that point, things got really bad and I began to question whether my research was worth this self-inflicted pain. Then, out of the blue, I was attacked by the leader of the retirement community's "Prayer Group." During the next nine minutes, this woman quickly approached the podium on a walker with outfitted with tennis balls to reduce the friction between her walking device and the ground below. I attempted to shout her down and to escape but she was too fast. The next thing you know, I was attacked. The last thing I remember, was that sweet lady extending her middle finger in my face and yelling, "Death to the A$% Clown."

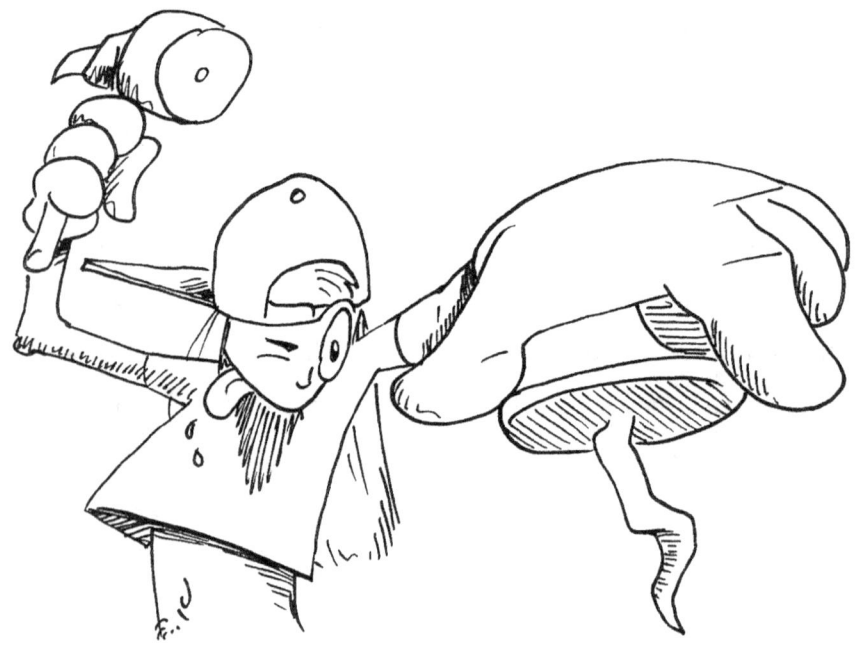

CHAPTER 21

WHAT NOBODY WANTS

Many people are in search of language that they can use that would put an end to the bickering and arguments that would quickly remove the tension and ill feelings between people. However, the quest that I am on, involves determining how to increase the bickering, the arguments and the tension between people, and so I'm a conflicted man. On one hand, I've learned the secrets of how to win friends and influence people, as a result of attempting to do just the opposite. Yet, still my sworn duty that I made to myself is to learn how to repel potential friends, employees, and customers, and how to not influence people.

Dale Carnegie, the best-selling author of *How to Win Friends and Influence People* once wrote, "I don't blame you one iota for feeling as you do. If I were you I would undoubtedly feel just as you do."

And so I thought for my research, I would commit to saying just the opposite when dealing with people, and the first opportunity I was presented with to demonstrate my mastery of how to repel potential friends, employees and customers occurred while trying to renew my driver's license.

After waiting in line for forty minutes behind a line of humans that smelled like a mixture between armpits and neglect, I finally made my way to the front of the line to renew my driver's license, and the man working my line said to me, "Sir how can I help you today?".

On a mission to repel potential friends, employees and customers I responded with, "I've been waiting in line behind the smelliest humans on the planet for the past forty minutes because you guys are short-staffed, yet again, despite your high prices."

He then said, "Well, sir I apologize for your wait, but how can I help you?".

At this point, I thought that it would be appropriate to bust out a little of my reverse How to Win Friends and Influence People technology by stating:

"I blame you 100% for making me wait. If I were you I would not tolerate big lines, slow service and soul-sucking smell of humanity. If I were you I would go at a pace that is 200% faster than the rate that you are moving at. By the way, have you taken a shower in the past 30 days?"

I was not allowed to renew my driver's license as a result of "some technicality." At that point, I wrote down in my "Man Journal" that you must not ever be sympathetic with the other person's ideas and desires if you want to repel friends, employees and customers.

The Epic Whale of a Tale Featuring America's Self-Proclaimed Most Humble Male

How to Repel Potential Friends and Not Influence People

CHAPTER 22

AN APPEAL THAT NOBODY LIKES

Back in the day, one of the world's most successful people was J. Pierpont Morgan. In fact, J.P. Morgan was the man who bought Carnegie Steel in 1901 for $480 million, which today would be $13 billion. Anyway, J.P. Morgan said that, "A person usually has two reasons for doing a thing; one that sounds good and a real one."

If you are hell-bent on how to win friends and influence people, you must appeal to a person's nobler motives, and thus you want to begin saying things like, "Mr. Smith, I know that you are a man of your word and not the kind of person that would simply refuse to ever pay me the remaining $8,000 for the new house that I built you, so let me ask you this, what is the payment plan that is going to work the best for you. Do you want to pay me $4,000 per month for the next two months, or do you want to pay me the remaining $8,000 all up front?"

However, if you want to repel potential friends, employees, and customers and to not influence people ever, I would highly recommend that you call out people for the bull sh#% that they are telling you. As an example, and to prove my strategy, I once got a job as a debt collector, and this is what I said to a dead-beat father in his 40's who continued to bounce checks to the rent-a-center type business that he leased-to-own his 72 inch TV from.

Me: "Hello, Is this Randy?"

Randy: "Yes, this is Randy. How can I help you?"

Me: "Randy, history shows that you are a diligent person in both your personal and financial life, so I wanted to ask you if your lazy a$# was going to make a payment this month, or if you had already used the money you owe us at the casino?"

Randy, "Are you kidding me? Who is this?"

Me: "Randy, this is Mr. Judgement Day, and right now, it looks at though you are on the fast track to hell. Good job on creating those kids during your moments of ecstasy. However, now it's time for you to actually pay for something that you bought for the first time in your life. So you do want me to put down on your file that you were unable to pay due to financial hardship, or because you got yet another woman that you met at the casino pregnant?"

Randy: "How did you know!? She wasn't supposed to tell anybody yet."

I didn't collect any money from Randy during that call, although that was my job at the time.

The Epic Whale of a Tale Featuring America's Self-Proclaimed Most Humble Male

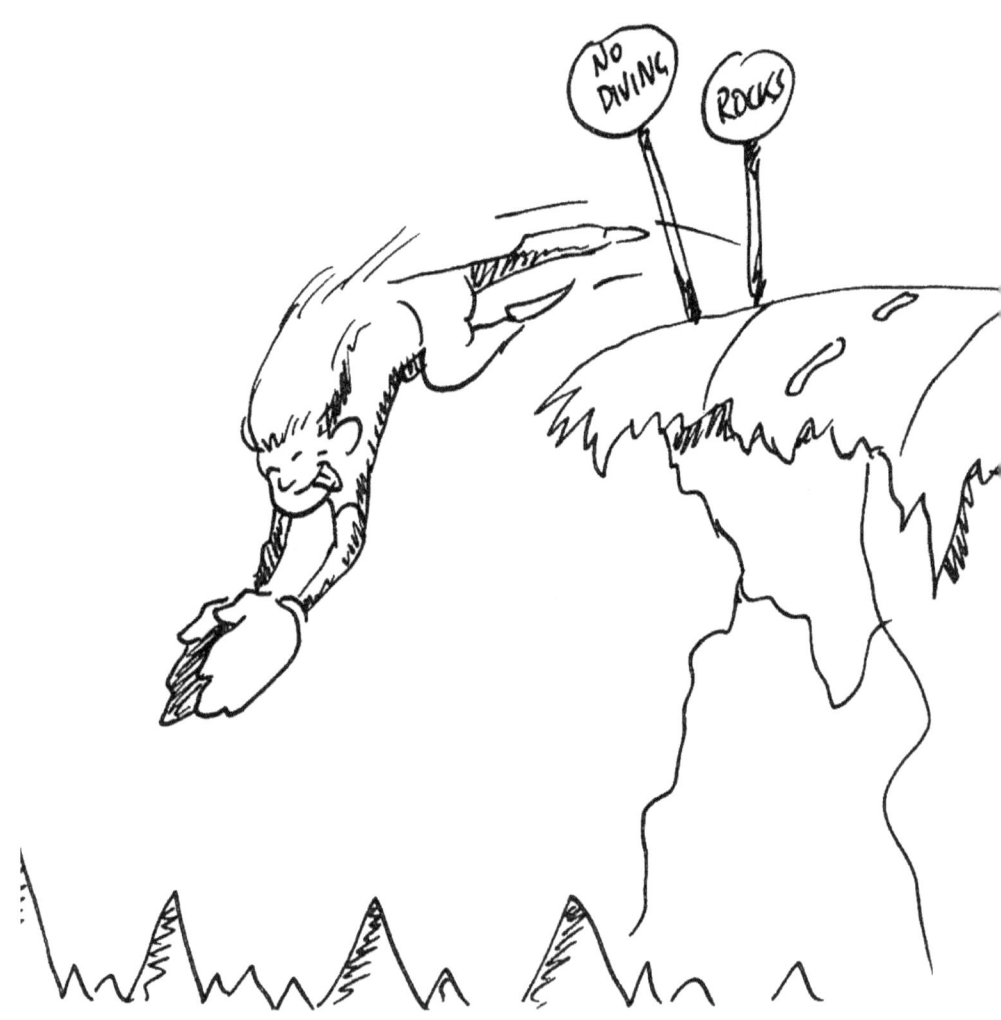

CHAPTER 23

THE MOVIES DON'T DO IT, BISHOP T.D. JAKES DOESN'T DO IT. SO WHY DON'T YOU TRY IT?

Although it has been proven time and time again, I will share with you a truth that has always been tough for me to grasp; the truth is never enough. In fact the truths that you want to share must be made vivid, dramatic and exciting or the people will reject your message no matter how true and valuable it is. This is the difference between what the growing Life Church and Pastor Craig Groeschel delivers each and every week during his sermons versus the what the steadily shrinking and declining, local Lutheran churches are delivering on a daily basis.

NOTABLE QUOTABLE

"What you want to do is you want to create an emotion that matches a truth or an idea to inspire your entrepreneurs to attempt something they haven't done before. I'd try or I'd find myself punching the air in some great movie cheering, you know, ready to go, take on the world and fight or whatever. And, and the emotion was very real. So what I wanted to do is I wanted to mix emotion with truth."

PASTOR CRAIG GROESCHEL

(The founding pastor of America's largest evangelical church, Life.Church)

And so to proudly demonstrate what happens when you absolutely refuse to mix truth with dramatic, vivid, and exciting content, I have secretly been leading the Lutheran Church (although I can't prove it) into the ground for years.

FUN FACT

"According to projections from the Evangelical Lutheran Church in America's (ELCA) Office of Research and Evaluation, the whole denomination will have fewer than 67,000 members in 2050, with fewer than 16,000 in worship on an average Sunday by 2041. That's right: according to current trends, the church will basically cease to exist within the next generation."

https://faithlead.luthersem.edu/decline/
https://news.gallup.com/poll/248837/church-membership-down-sharply-past-two-decades.aspx

http://www.startribune.com/readers-write-the-unchurching-of-america/488152081/

https://www.weau.com/content/news/Fewer-Wisconsinites-are-attending-church-564131841.html

---

The Epic Whale of a Tale Featuring America's Self-Proclaimed Most Humble Male

How to Repel Potential Friends and Not Influence People

CHAPTER 24

WHEN SOMETHING IS NOT WORKING, STAY LOYAL TO IT

Although I don't understand why many people choose to believe this way, I have found that when something is not working, most people stay loyal to it. In fact, while doing my research for this book I have found that most people are wrong about almost everything most of the time including:

- Most people believe it's okay to steal from their workplace.

FUN FACT

"75% of employees steal from the workplace and most do so repeatedly."

https://www.cbsnews.com/news/employee-theft-are-you-blind-to-it/

- Most people believe that it's okay to cheat on their spouse.

FUN FACT

"78 percent of the men interviewed had cheated on their current partner."

— 5 MYTHS ABOUT CHEATING

https://www.washingtonpost.com/opinions/five-myths-about-cheating/2012/02/08/gIQANGdaBR_story.html?noredirect=on&utm_term=.05ab54a87466

- Most people believe that is alright and 100% okay to make things up on their resumes.

FUN FACT

"85% of job applicants lie on resumes."

INC. MAGAZINE

https://www.inc.com/jt-odonnell/staggering-85-of-job-applicants-lying-on-resumes-.html

And thus, for your benefit and for my research, I landed a job at a local men's salon working as the front desk person where I committed myself to always acting as though I did not want to be there, and would be counting down the minutes until my shift was over and I would be free again. In fact, during one particular customer interaction, I remember it like it was yesterday.

Jeff "The Customer" - "Hey, so how are things going?"

Me - "Well, thank the Lord, I'm almost done with my shift."

Jeff "The Customer" - "So what's going on?"

Me - "Well corporate has its head up its a#& and all I do every day is the same crap. I'm just sick and tired of being sick and tired. But anyway, what was your name and I'll get you all signed in Mark?"

The customer did not come back very often after that interaction.

CHAPTER 25

BE A TROLL: HOW TO NOT CHANGE PEOPLE WHILE GIVING GREAT OFFENSE AND STIRRING UP RESENTMENT

Whenever you must deliver direct constructive criticism to someone, make sure that you first go out of your way to compliment them, and then after the constructive criticism has been delivered, make sure that you conclude the interaction with yet another piece of praise. Remember that the "hug, kick, hug" is the formula that you must follow to deliver the kind of constructive criticism needed to save lives, companies, organizations and families. To better illustrate this point, I have chosen to include the letter that President Abraham Lincoln wrote to General Hooker during the Civil War.

```
Major General Hooker:

General,

I have placed you at the head of the
Army of the Potomac. Of course I have
done this upon what appear to me to be
sufficient reasons. And yet I think it
best for you to know that there are some
```

things in regard to which, I am not quite satisfied with you. I believe you to be a brave and a skillful soldier, which, of course, I like. I also believe you do not mix politics with your profession, in which you are right. You have confidence in yourself, which is a valuable, if not an indispensable quality. You are ambitious, which, within reasonable bounds, does good rather than harm. But I think that during Gen. Burnside's command of the Army, you have taken counsel of your ambition, and thwarted him as much as you could, in which you did a great wrong to the country, and to a most meritorious and honorable brother officer.

I have heard, in such away as to believe it, of your recently saying that both the Army and the Government needed a Dictator. Of course it was not for this, but in spite of it, that I have given you the command. Only those generals who gain successes, can set up dictators. What

I now ask of you is military success, and I will risk the dictatorship. The government will support you to the utmost of its' ability, which is neither more nor less than it has done and will do for all commanders.

I much fear that the spirit which you have aided to infuse into the Army, of criticizing their Commander, and withholding confidence from him, will now turn upon you. I shall assist you as far as I can, to put it down.

Neither you, nor Napoleon, if he were alive again, could get any good out of an army, while such a spirit prevails in it.

And now, beware of rashness. Beware of rashness, but with energy, and sleepless vigilance, go forward, and give us victories.

Yours very truly,
A. Lincoln

How to Repel Potential Friends and Not Influence People

CHAPTER 26

IF YOU MUST FIND FAULT, START OFF BY OFFENDING THE OTHER PARTY.

Many humans on the planet earth begin to provide criticism after providing sincere praise and using the word "but" before providing a soul-sucking, social-armor-piercing-and-relationship-changing-piece-of-constructive-criticism. As an example, some people might say, "Madison, we are so excited for you and we are glad that you earned that scholarship, but, we have concerns about your promiscuity."

The moment that you and I say "but," it truly does make an ass out of you and me.

However, my research is 100% dedicated to offending the other party, and to repel potential employees, customers, and everyone and thus I would recommend that you would use the word "but" as much as possible after anybody says anything to you. If saying, "yeah but" after every statement that anybody says to you fails to kill all rapport you have with people, I recommend that you interrupt them as a they are speaking to say to "yeah but" before deep diving into a strongly held opinion that you have that is in 100% opposition of what the person you are talking to is saying.

In fact, in order to help you take your life to the next level, I have consistently forced myself to interrupt friends, employees, current customers and potential customers with the phrase, "Yeah, but."

In fact, just a few weeks ago, a member of my team told me that they were sincerely excited about watching the Kansas City Chiefs play against the San Francisco 49ers in this year's Super Bowl.

And I responded with, "Yeah, but isn't soccer really the most popular sport in America?"

He responded kindly with, "Claytron, I really do understand what you are saying, however the statistics don't lie. More people around the world are playing soccer than any other sport."

I responded with, "Everything you said is correct, but you are 100% wrong about 100% of what you just said."

This conversation did not go well.

The Epic Whale of a Tale Featuring America's Self-Proclaimed Most Humble Male

How to Repel Potential Friends and Not Influence People

CHAPTER 27

FOCUS ON WHAT THEY DID WRONG AND NEVER MENTION WHAT YOU HAVE EVER DONE WRONG

In his internationally best-selling book *How to Win Friends and Influence People*, Dale Carnegie writes, "Talk about your own mistakes before criticizing the other person." And so to demonstrate my loyalty to my research, I needed to complete *How to Repel Friends, Employees, Customer and to Influence People*, once upon a time, I chose to land yet another job working at a large big box fitness gym. I can remember it like it was yesterday.

Day one at a job can always be a little awkward. You don't really know anybody, you don't really know where everything is located, you don't know how the software works, and you haven't been there long enough to establish any rapport with your co-workers yet. However, I found that this situation provided me fertile ground with which to conduct my research on what happens when you focus on only what "they" did wrong, and never mention what you have ever done wrong.

My shift started at 9:00 AM, so I arrived at work at 8:30 AM. I went to the locker room to put on my brand-new athletic company polo shirt, my magnet name tag, and then I looked into the mirror and said "well done" loud enough so that everybody could hear me as I finished combing my hair, and then I strolled out to the front desk at 8:40 AM. At 8:50, my manager came up to introduce himself. He said, Hey Claytron, we're glad you are here. We'll have the all-staff morning huddle here at 9:30 AM, but you can go ahead and get started by folding these towels and then Samantha will be here at 9:00 to teach you how to check-in and check-out our members. Sound good?"

I replied, "Absolutely."

At 9:02, Samantha strolled in and I greeted her, "Hi, are you Samantha!?"

She replied, "Yes. Are you Claytron? I heard you were going to be starting today."

With great joy, "Yes. I'm Claytron. It looks like you are running a little behind. Do you need a hand carrying your athletic bags?"

She said, "No."

I said, "Hey, and I noticed you aren't wearing your nametag, did you forget it at home as you were rushing out?! You know, I always say you are either 15 minutes early or 15 minutes late."

She glared at me.

I then said, "Oh, don't worry about it. In fact, Business Insider now shows that 19% of Americans are just like you."

FUN FACT

https://www.businessinsider.com/these-are-the-americans-who-are-always-late-to-work-2015-3

She said, "What are you talking about?"

I said, "Oh, I mean an article in Business Insiders showed that a staggering 19% of Americans are LATE-EES."

She retorted, "19% of America's are ladies?"

I said jokingly, "No, not ladies. I mean LATE-EES. Mr. and Mrs. Lates-Alot. You know, the kind of people that are always late like YOU."

Day one was my first and last day.

How to Repel Potential Friends and Not Influence People

CHAPTER 28

CREATE A YELP! ACCOUNT AND INVEST HOURS AND HOURS INTO BECOMING A SELF-PROCLAIMED RESTAURANT SNOB

In order for you to become a super-successful person, you must learn how to focus exclusively on revenue creating activities, and the action steps that are going to help you gain traction in this world of perpetual distraction. However, if you are not looking to grow and improve the overall profitability of your company as a result of providing more solutions to the problems being experienced by your ideal and likely buyer, then this chapter is for you.

While experiencing the most non-profitable times of my life, and in the course of the non-lucrative years that I spent going in the wrong direction daily, I can tell you that the following things mattered to me most each and every day:

Although at times it has been tempting to be productive, I've chosen to waste this time for you the reader. In fact, I invested at least one solid half hour per day to updating my Yelp account with page after page of scathing reviews about the businesses owned and operated by others.

Although, I could have invested the time needed to improve myself, to earn an income, and to save the money needed to eventually open up my own business. I have chosen to take the low road for you the reader to demonstrate the 100% truth about how to *How to Repel Potential Friends and Not Influence People*.

Investing forty five minutes per day to upload photos of my food and posting them on Facebook, Instagram, Twitter, Snapchat, Yelp and the local business owner's Google Maps page along with yet another scathing Google review.

One of my best tips for losing big in the game of business and life has been to argue with business owners online about the poor level of service that they provide instead of trying to become literally non-poor as a result of actually getting a job.

The Epic Whale of a Tale Featuring America's Self-Proclaimed Most Humble Male

How to Repel Potential Friends and Not Influence People

CHAPTER 29

NO ONE LIKES TO TAKE ORDERS, SO GIVE ORDERS TO PEOPLE YOU JUST MET, PEOPLE YOU HAVE NO RAPPORT WITH AND PEOPLE WHO YOU ARE NOT IN CHARGE OF

A ton of orders

The legendary personal communication expert Dale Carnegie once famously wrote, "asking questions not only make an order more palatable, it often stimulates the creativity of the persons whom you ask. People are more likely to accept an order if they have a part in the decision that caused the order to be issued. However, Dale didn't ever "seem to have the time" needed to test whether the reverse of this universal communication truth was also true did he? No he didn't. So, I knew that if it was meant to be, it was going to be up to me to prove once and for all that no one likes to take orders. So give orders to people you just met, and people whom you have no rapport with, and to people who you are not in charge of.

My research lead me back to another local grocery store, where I found the sushi guy hard at work rolling fresh sushi. It was there in the sushi section over by the deli section and the "meat carver guy" that my research began.

I calmly said, "Excuse me sir. I think you may be rolling those sushi rolls wrong."

Shocked by what I had said, the super-kind, hard-at-work sushi guy dressed in his white chef's outfit said, "Excuse me. What did you say?", with a smile on his face. I told him, "Listen here buddy you heard me. Don't play the game. I said, I think you are rolling that sushi the wrong way."

He looked at me, and said, "Sir, I've been master trained in the art of sushi for over twenty years, and I appreciate your concern, but could I help you with something."

I snapped back, "Listen dude, I'm here to help, and from what I can tell you do not have a rubber mat to stand on, and with posture like that you are going to be looking like Gollum from Lord of the Rings at the age of sixty. Stand up straight, and get a rubber mat. Have some pride for yourself! Geez."

The previously calm sushi king then looked at me as though he was going to kill me with one of his sushi knives and he said, "Buddy, I don't want to have any problems. Do you want to order some sushi, or are you just here to cause issues."

I told him this, and this is what I told him. "Dude. I just care about your hunched over spine and your body that you are destroying by not standing on a rubber mat. You my friend must have low self-esteem, because your posture is just bad."

It was at this time, when he physically assaulted me that I finally had the confirmation that I needed to prove that things go bad when you give orders to people you just met, people whom you have no rapport with, and to people who you are not in charge of.

How to Repel Potential Friends and Not Influence People

CHAPTER 30

DON'T EVER LET THE OTHER PERSON SAVE FACE

Dale Carnegie once famously wrote, "Few of us ever stop to think. We ride roughshod over the feelings of others, getting our own way, finding fault, issuing threats, criticizing a child or an employee in front of others, without even considering the hurt to the other person's pride. Whereas a few minutes' thought, a considerate word or two, a genuine understanding of the other person's attitude, would go so far toward alleviating the sting."

And that are nifty words written by a modern day sage who was afraid to test out the theories of what really repels potential friends, employees and customers, and what absolutely is guaranteed to not influence people.

And so as I sat down on the metal bleachers to watch my daughter play a third-grade soccer game, I knew soon I would find the perfect opportunity to test my theories on what happens when you don't ever let the other person save face. As the game concluded, the girls went out to the center of the soccer field to shake hands, and to thank each other for being good sports, However, during the handshaking process, the head coach of the other team, and our head coach seemed to have a few not-so-nice-things to say to each other. I'm not a lip reader, but I could tell that neither party was too happy with the other following the game. I knew had something to work with. So, as our head coach walked back to the sideline, I thought that would be a perfect opportunity to verbally correct him for not setting the standard of sportsmanship that our third grade girls should aspire to.

The coach said to the team, "Amanda, that was a hell of a game. Those were great goals!"

Then, I interrupted with that painful correction that I knew he needed, "Hey coach. Sorry to interrupt, and with all due respect, I didn't appreciate the way you spoke to the other coach there at the end of the game. I could see the words that were coming out of your mouth you know."

The coach nicely said, "Well Claytron, I apologize I got heated out there. The other team however needs to know that you can't dropkick members of our team with their cleats every time they want to steal the ball. Hamilton (one of the third grade players) and Madison (one of the third grade players) both look like their legs have been attacked by a weed eater."

I said, "Well coach, that's why we pay you to coach our girls on this traveling team. You are out there setting a bad standard, and frankly one that we should all be ashamed of."

The coach apologized, "Mr. Menendez, please accept my apologies."

I said, "Sure, but what are you apologizing for? Are you apologizing for cursing out the other coach, for setting a bad example ,or for losing more games that you have won last year?"

The coach had to be held back as he attempted to punch me in the face.

The Epic Whale of a Tale Featuring America's Self-Proclaimed Most Humble Male

How to Repel Potential Friends and Not Influence People

CHAPTER 31

HOW TO SPUR PEOPLE ONTO FAILURE

Research done by Dale Carnegie and other leading authors in the world on the subject of emotional intelligence, including the *New York Times* best-selling author of Emotional Intelligence, Daniel Goleman instructs us to praise people when possible because humans on the earth respond to emotional events much more quickly than to logical events. So, unless you want to find yourself chronically jobless and in physical pain, it would make much more sense to praise people when possible, as opposed to constantly condemning and birrating people.

NOTABLE QUOTABLE

"The emotional brain responds to an event more quickly than the thinking brain."

DANIEL GOLEMAN

(The New York Times best-selling author of Emotional Intelligence and a ThrivetimeShow.com podcast guest)

"If your emotional abilities aren't in hand, if you don't have self-awareness, if you are not able to manage your distressing emotions, if you can't have empathy and have effective relationships, then no matter how smart you are, you are not going to get very far."

DANIEL GOLEMAN

(The New York Times best-selling author of Emotional Intelligence and a ThrivetimeShow.com podcast guest)

However, I'm not interested in being just another talking head and author who simply regurgitates timeless truths time and time again. No. I'm on a quest to be the best in the world when it comes to proving the specific steps that you must take to repel potential friends, employees, and customers, and to not influence anyone. I once landed a job at a local drug store as a cashier where I mentally committed myself to critiquing every customer, without ever saying a positive thing. Because I wanted to know first-hand what would happen to man who never said nice things to people ever. How long would it take to get yelled at, fired and hated by everyone? Two days? Two hours? Two minutes? These are the questions I ponder day in and day out.

Day one at that drug store was a rough one.

As my first customer approached the checkout line, I repeated my inner dialogue and my mantra silently to myself saying in my mind only, "Condemnation is your conversation...Condemnation is your obligation... Condemnation is your conversation...Condemnation is your obligation...".

I said, "Mam, can I help you check out?"

The sweet brunette woman in what appeared to be her mid-thirties said, "Yes, thank you."

I responded, "Well, don't get too excited."

She said, "What?"

I said, "The words that just came out of my mouth were, "Don't get too excited lady'!"

She rolled her eyes and searched my face with her eyes to see if I was kidding.

I looked back upon her angrily, with squinted eyes filled with extreme judgment and with a look of total condemnation.

She said, "Are we a little upset today?"

I said, "I'm upset. I don't know if (we) are upset. We just met. What? Now we are supposed to share emotional bonds and feelings that I don't even share with my wife. Lady, that's weird!"

She said, "What is wrong with you?"

I attempted to show her the ten year rash I've had just above my left nipple, and she ran out screaming, "Creep."

My boss saw the situation, watched the videotape of the situation and immediately fired me. Aha! I had my data and it only took me four minutes to prove my theory that when you constantly condemn people, you cannot possibly become successful.

How to Repel Potential Friends and Not Influence People

CHAPTER 32

THE BIG SECRET OF REPELLING PEOPLE

If you want to make sure that people hate you, loathe you, and dislike you as their manager, boss or supervisor, point out to them first and foremost that they have to do what you are telling them because you are their boss. Constantly refer to your title, and don't spend any time getting the other person to actually want to do the task that you need them to do.

During the course of my research, I landed a job at a local hair salon where I was hired to be the "front desk" jockey. This didn't go well during the first two weeks, and then one day it happened. My manager lost it. Yes. My direct manager ran out of the building screaming and babbling (maybe "speaking in tongues") something to the effect of, "YOU have caused me to hate the only job that I have ever loved! I quit!" before storming out of the building to never be seen or heard from again. So for a moment by default I became the new manager, because the "front desk" position was viewed internally to be the step in the organizational chart, that preceded becoming a manager.

I sprung into action like a PUMA, and I gathered for four ladies who were working the shift and said, "My fellow teammates it is not a time to bicker, to question or to lament the loss of your boss of twelve years. No, now is the time to ask not what I can do for you as your manager, but it is now time to ask yourself, what can you do for me?!"

Then, I was rudely interrupted by one of the veteran stylists by the name of Kymber who said, "You just ran off the best manager I've ever had. That's not cool man!"

Claytron Menedez: "Well sweetheart, where there is smoke there is fire if you know what I mean."

Kymber: "No I don't. What happened!?"

Claytron Menedez: "What happened was a little lady by the name of Kymber just raised her voice to her new boss. And now a big manager man by the name of Claytron Menendez just now got out a write up slip to write her up for insubordination. That's what happened during this conversation! Do you hear me?! I'm your manager."

Kymber: "Well, I quit."

Claytron Menedez: "Well good. Because I would rather cut hair without you. Management was put in place to manage you. Right ladies?!"

Carla: I quit too.

Claytron Menedez: "Oh, you quit? Sure you quit, like Ricki Lake and Kirstie Alley quit eating chips?!"

Carla: You are jerk Claytron! And your name is weird. I quit!"

Claytron Menedez: "Listen ladies. Has a pope ever resigned from his God appointed position when things got tough?!"

Alley: "Yes! I'm Catholic. Pope Benedict XVI resigned on February 28th of 2013 due to his declining health due to old age."

Claytron Menendez: "Okay. That's one point for you, but did James Bowie and Davy Crockett quit while defending the Alamo against Santa Anna's Mexican army?!"

Alley: "No! But they all died. And I'm not going to die here with you. You're an idiot!"

Claytron Menendez: "Alley, no! You can't quit, you've always been the hottest stylist. You know that I have favored you!"

Alley: "You'll be hearing from my lawyer! And I quit!"

And Then the final team member felt the momentum pulling her to quit, and so she quit while following the other three stylists out the door and yelling something that sounded like "Turn in Bell! You mother trucker!".

CHAPTER 33

NEVER SAVE MONEY AND ALWAYS LIVE ABOVE YOUR MEANS

During this past decade that I have devoted to attempting to *Repel Potential Friends and Not Influence People*, I have discovered nearly all successful people save money, and choose to live below their means, and to delay gratification in order to save that money. However, I have also noticed that regardless of how much money they earn, people who repel potential friends and who do not influence people seem to be obsessed with spending all of their money, 100% of the time to create financially urgent events and a nearly endless desire to get rich quick.

NOTABLE QUOTABLE

"If you cannot save money, then the seeds of greatness are not in you." If you cannot save money, then the seeds of greatness are not in you."

W. CLEMENT STONE

(The self-help author, and entrepreneur who founded Combined Insurance Company of America, after reading Napoleon Hill's Think and Grow Rich. The Combined Insurance company provided both accident and health insurance coverage and by 1930, employed over 1,000 agents who sold insurance all across these great United States. By 1979, his insurance company exceeded $1 billion in assets.)

NOTABLE QUOTABLE

"Wealth from get-rich-quick schemes quickly disappears; wealth from hard work grows over time."

PROVERBS 13:11

(New Living Translation)

FUN FACT

"Fed survey shows 40 percent of adults still can't cover a $400 emergency expense."

https://www.cnbc.com/2018/05/22/fed-survey-40-percent-of-adults-cant-cover-400-emergency-expense.html

---

NOTABLE QUOTABLE

"The sluggard does not plow after the autumn, So he begs during the harvest and has nothing."

PROVERBS 20:4

NOTABLE QUOTABLE

"Poor is he who works with a negligent hand. But the hand of the diligent makes rich. He who gathers in summer is a son who acts wisely, But he who sleeps in harvest is a son who acts shamefully."

PROVERBS 10:4-5

Thus, I decided to throw logic away during this past decade, to always live above my means, and to buy as much crap as big-box retailers were willing to sell me. In fact, one day I went into a massive furniture store and asked the sales associate what I needed to do to buy the biggest television that I have ever seen in my life. In fact, the television was so massive, that I almost wept when I first saw it for the first time. It was a 98" inch TV produced by Sony and the sales associate let me know that it would only cost me $2,500 per month if I qualified to buy it. I told the sales associate to, "Let her rip."

The sales associate asked me, "What does that mean?"

I turned to him with a look of contempt and said, "What do you think it means? See if I qualify for it?! You know I'm never going to pay that off. It's like my student loans, it's just a massive amount of money that I am borrowing to have a good time that I never intend on paying back. Go and see if I qualify for it my man!"

The sales associate returned several minutes later to let me know both the good news and the bad news.

Sales associate: "Sir, unfortunately you do not qualify to buy the $59,999 Sony - 98" Class - LED - Z9G Master Series television that you applied for. However, I am showing that you do qualify to buy the 86" Class LG - LED Smart TV which is currently on sale for only $1,899.99. Thus, your monthly payment would only be $158.34 per month. Would that work for you?"

Me: "Look, buddy, we are living in the "End Times." We've lived through Y2K, 9/11, the Anthrax Scare, the Swine Flu Epidemic, the West Nile Virus, and now the Coronavirus. Everyday we live is just a bonus round that defies my emotionally-based world view. I must buy it now using money that I cannot afford in the future to impress people I don't really know. Buy it now!"

This television was repossessed a few months later, but it was sweet to have during those 9 weeks of ecstasy as I called in sick to work 5 times in those 9 weeks in order to watch every movie that I love that I had never had the opportunity to previously watch on an 86" TV in the past.

The Epic Whale of a Tale Featuring America's Self-Proclaimed Most Humble Male

How to Repel Potential Friends and Not Influence People

CHAPTER 34

PRACTICE POOR HYGIENE WHEN THE BOSS IS NOT LOOKING

During this decade of dysfunction that I have suffered through for your benefit, I have discovered that the people that practice the best hygiene, on average, get ahead and those that attempt to not take a shower when the person in power is out of town, tend to lose. You see, even if applied properly, dry shampoo will leave hair looking oily and gross, and when you look homeless, oily, and gross, you repel people the most and that is where the research and the personal sacrifice that I was willing to put into this book reached its limits (even for me).

Normally, I have always taken a shower once per day. However, for the benefit of YOU - the reader I decided that I would only take a shower every four days in order to prove my theories on *How to Repel Friends and Not Influence People*, and I landed a job at a jewelry store, just to prove how powerful your personal appearance can be.

I arrived at work early on day one of my job at the jewelry store, knowing that I had not taken a shower in four days, and knowing that objectively, I really smelled bad by any standard. Despite having had the time needed to take a shower and to brush my teeth, I chose not to do so for the benefit of you the reader and things didn't go well. At this jewelry store, our boss believed that "every potential customer was important" and so he always staffed three jewelry salespeople to work during every shift, and he claimed that Saturdays were the best days for selling jewelry. However, during my first Saturday, I found that once somebody got within about two to three feet of me, they smelled poverty or they saw general negligence in my appearance, and chose to talk to one of the other two sales associates each and every time. And it was then, that I discovered that when you both look and smell bad, you may never, ever sell anything to anyone.

The Epic Whale of a Tale Featuring America's Self-Proclaimed Most Humble Male

CHAPTER 35

CONCLUSION: CHOOSING TO REMAIN POOR REQUIRES A COMMITMENT TO JACKASSERY

My friend, being perpetually poor while winning the genetic lottery and having been born in these great United States, requires a commitment to "Jackassery." If you want to stay poor, you must commit to living by the code the 10 Commandments of Jackassery that I have dedicated a decade of my life to researching.

Commandment #1 - Never show up on time and always have an excuse that you actually believe for being late.

Commandment #2 - 30% of the time, do not do what you say you are going to do. This will kill the confidence of all people that were on the fence about doing business with you, promoting you, and trusting you.

Commandment #3 - Practice poor hygiene. See how long you can go without bathing, showering, and brushing your teeth before your boss has to point it out to you that you have to take a shower now, or you will be fired.

Commandment #4 - Always do slightly less than you are supposed to do. This will allow the level of trust that you have gained from others to be eroded slowly over time.

Commandment #5 - Live above your means and never save money. For all that is holy, never save money, because when you do this, you begin to develop good financial habits, and you may actually start to get ahead.

Commandment #6 - Gamble whenever possible. When you gamble your hard-earned money you showcase your commitment to remaining poor and that is important if you want to remain poor.

Commandment #7 - Spend as much time as possible per day angrily debating religion and politics on social media, and this will ensure that you will never have the time needed to actually improve your life.

Commandment #8 - Never read books. In fact, this should be the last book that you ever read if you want to remain poor. Research clearly shows that the readers are the leaders so you must make a clean break here. You must resolve in your mind to never ever read a book that teaches you the practical skills that you need to pay the bills ever again.

Commandment #9 - Always ask God to do the things that you should do yourself. Instead of actually applying for a job, ask God to give you a great job. Instead of actually studying to pass a test, ask God to help grant you the wisdom needed to pass the test. Instead of saving the money needed to start a business, ask God to give you the money you need to buy real estate you are wanting to buy.

Commandment #10 - Commit to only investing in things that sound like a get-rich-quick scheme. You must choose now to only invest in pyramid schemes, multi-level marketing scams, and things that sound too good to be true.

SAYING GOODBYE IS NEVER EASY TO DO:

As I wrap up this book, I feel like I'm saying goodbye to a good friend, and to a way of life that has proven to not produce success, but to a way of life that I have been habitually loyal to. I feel like I've been a card carrying member of the socialist party who has seen socialism and communism fail in Cuba, North Korea, the former U.S.S.R., and Venezuela. I now know the facts about the poverty causing pain associated with repelling potential friends, and how to not to influence people, but I'm addicted to it. It's like being a cigarette smoker who knows that their ways will eventually kill them, yet they simply choose to not stop smoking because they are addicted to it. So as for me, I continue on repelling potential friends and not influencing people because that is what I am now good at. So, if you would like to get a signed copy of this book, please meet me under the bridge located at the intersection of highway 169 and 71st street in Tulsa. I'll be there waiting for you with my stolen shopping cart, my Sharpie marker, and my cardboard that proclaims perhaps that most false advertising message of all-time, "Will Work for Food."

How to Repel Potential Friends and Not Influence People

WANT TO KNOW EVEN MORE?
CHECK OUT ALL OF CLAY'S BOOKS

START HERE
The World's Best Business Growth & Consulting Book: Business Growth Strategies from the World's Best Business Coach.

DON'T LET YOUR EMPLOYEES HOLD YOU HOSTAGE
This candid book shares how to avoid being held hostage by employees.

THE ENTREPRENEUR'S DRAGON ENERGY
The Mindset Kanye, Trump and You Need to Succeed.

BOOM
The 14 Proven Steps to Business Success.

JACKASSARY
Jackassery will serve as a beacon of light for other entrepreneurs that are looking to avoid troublesome employees and difficult situations. This is real. This is raw. This is unfiltered entrepreneurship.

THE ART OF GETTING THINGS DONE
Clay Clark breaks down the proven, time-tested and time freedom creating super moves that you can use to create both the time freedom and financial freedom that most people only dream about.

THRIVE
How to Take Control of Your Destiny and Move Beyond Surviving... Now!

MANAGEMENT IS MENTORSHIP
9 Big Ideas for Effectively Managing Your Business in an Increasingly Dumb, Distracted & Dishonest America

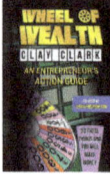

WHEEL OF WEALTH
An Entrepreneur's Action Guide.

SEARCH ENGINE DOMINATION
Learn the Proven System We've Used to Earn Millions.

The Epic Whale of a Tale Featuring America's Self-Proclaimed Most Humble Male

MAKE YOUR LIFE EPIC
Clay shares his journey and struggle from the dorm room to the board room during his raw and action-packed story of how he built DJConnection.com.

PODCAST DOMINATION 101
This book will show you how to prepare, record, luanc, and begin generating income from your podcast, all from your home studio!

F6 JOURNAL
Meta Thrive Time Journal.

TRADE-UPS
Learn how to design and live the life you love, how to find and create the time needed to get things done in a world filled with endless digital distractions, and more!

IF MY WALLS COULD TALK
The Notes, Quotes, & Epiphanies I've Written On Clay's Office Walls. (Hardcover)

IT'S NOT LONELY AT THE TOP
15 Keys to achieving a successful, peaceful, and drama-free life.

(3/4 of this book is handwritten by Clay Clark, himself)

SALES DOMINATION
Clay Clark is a master of selling and now he wants to teach you his proven processes, scalable systems and sales mastery moves in a humorous and practical way.

How to Repel Potential Friends and Not Influence People